CEREMONIES
OF THE SEASONS

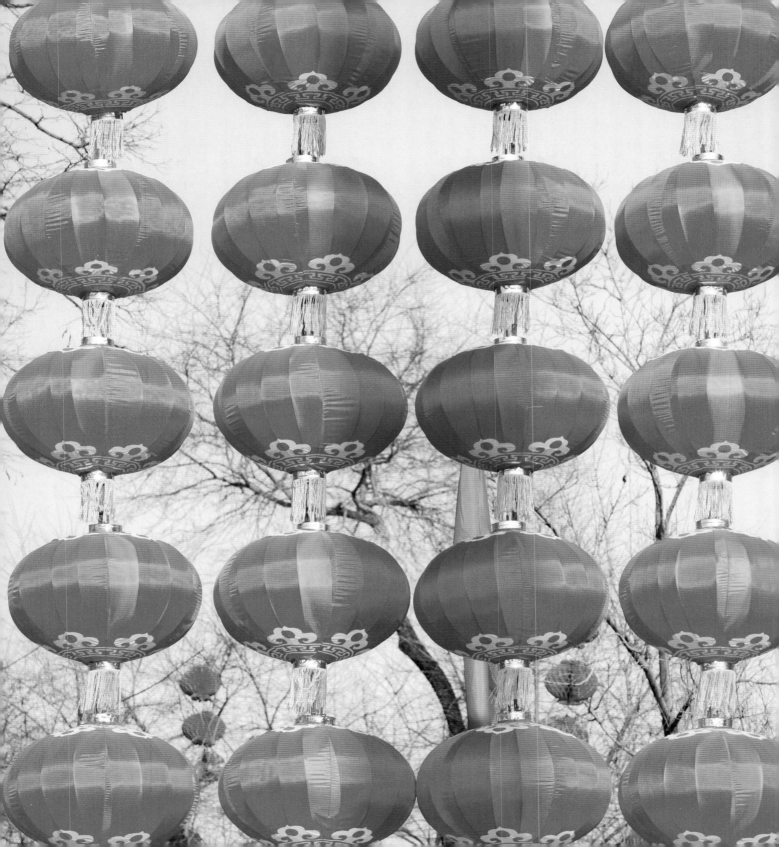

CEREMONIES
OF THE SEASONS

JENNIFER COLE

EXPLORING AND CELEBRATING
NATURE'S ETERNAL CYCLE

DUNCAN BAIRD PUBLISHERS

LONDON

Ceremonies of the Seasons
Jennifer Cole

This edition first published in the UK and USA in 2007 by
Duncan Baird Publishers Ltd
Sixth Floor, Castle House
75–76 Wells Street
London W1T 3QH

Conceived, created and designed by Duncan Baird Publishers

Managing Designer: Suzanne Tuhrim
Designer: Gail Jones
Managing Editor: Kelly Thompson
Editor: Zoë Fargher
Editorial Assistants: Emma Maule, Kirty Topiwala
Picture Researcher: Louise Glasson
Consultant: Juliette Wood
Commissioned artwork: Sally Taylor

Library of Congress Cataloging-in-Publication Data Available

ISBN: 978-1-84483-463-1

10 9 8 7 6 5 4 3 2 1

Typeset in Liberty and Perpetua
Color reproduction by Colourscan, Singapore
Printed in China

NOTE
The abbreviations BCE and CE are used throughout this book:
BCE Before the Common Era (the equivalent of BC)

"What incomes have we not had from a flower, and how unfailing are the dividends of the seasons?"

JAMES RUSSELL LOWELL (1819–1891)

Contents

· · · · ·

Introduction 8

Why Do We Celebrate? 8

Seasonal and Sacred Calendars 12

Cycles of Sun and Moon 14

Solstices and Equinoxes 16

Understanding the Ancient Year 18

Winter turns to Spring 22

Emergence 24

First Flowers 26

Brighid, the Bright One 28

Candlemas 30

Chinese New Year 32

Groundhog Day 33

Love Festivals 34

Spring 36

Spring Equinox 38

New Beginnings 40

The Roots of Modern Easter 42

Festivals of Colour, Love and
    Motherhood 46

Spring Storms and the Wind Flower 48

Resurrected Gods 50

Spring turns to Summer 52

May Day 54

A Blanket of Flowers 56

Banishing the Darkness 58

Hawthorn: the Fairy Tree 60

Horned Gods and May Games 62

The Green Man 64

Summer 66

Summer Solstice 68

Sun, Light and Fire 70

Summer in the Zodiac 74

A Time to Pause 76

The Oak: King of the Woods 78

Solstice Sites 80

Summer turns to Autumn 82

Harvest 84

Remembering Ancestors 86

Crop Deities: Myth and Ritual 88

Lughnasadh 92

Sheaf Ceremonies 94

Death and Rebirth 96

Autumn 98
  Autumn Equinox 100
  Marking Equinox and Harvest 102
  Rosh Hashanah to Sukkot 104
  Moon Cakes and Lanterns 106
  Celebrating the Vines 108
  Dying Light 110

Autumn turns to Winter 112
  Twilight 114
  Thanksgiving and Feasts of Plenty 116
  Days and Nights of the Dead 118
  Bonfire Nights 122
  Diwali 126

Winter 128
  Winter Solstice 130
  The Light Returns 132
  The Arrival of Father Christmas 134
  Yule Logs and Christmas Trees 136
  Chaos and Misrule 140
  Renewing the Cycle 142
  Winter and the Underworld 143

For reference
  Zodiac Months 144
  The Tree Calendar 146
  Cherokee Moon Months 148
  Glossary 150
  Further Reading 154
  Index 155
  Picture Credits and
    Acknowledgments 160

Why Do We Celebrate?

Since prehistory we have marked the year's landmarks with festivals and ceremonies, which often share certain key themes — despite vast cultural differences.

• • • • •

All calendars are founded upon a wish to organize our experience of time into manageable units — especially the year, with its recognizable seasonal landmarks. The natural rhythms of the world (the contrast of night and day, the changes of seasons and the cycles of the moon), and repeated events in nature (the ebbing and flowing of tides, the migrations of animals and birds), present a curious contradiction: on the one hand, constant change all around us; on the other, reliable repetition at regular intervals.

Calendars help us make sense of these cycles, reflecting various rhythms — seasonal, social and religious — within the structure of an ordered year that satisfies civic requirements. Important times within the year — such as tasks in the routine of farming, commemorations of important events or observable astronomical phenomena — are marked by celebrations, forming a rich pattern of ceremonial activity across diverse cultures. But *why* do we mark these calendrical highlights with elaborate rituals, and why are these celebrations often so similar in different societies and at different periods in human history?

MOVEABLE FEASTS

Festivals offer an opportunity for communal gathering and rejoicing on a local, national and even international level. Immigrant communities carry their own customs to new destinations, and their continued practice of beloved traditions maintains a link with their homeland and original culture. In the Antipodes, for example, European-style Christmas is still celebrated on December 25, even though in the southern hemisphere it coincides with the Summer rather than the Winter Solstice. And the Hindu festival of lights, Diwali, is celebrated today throughout Britain and the USA, alongside other Autumn customs such as Hallowe'en.

Diwali and Hallowe'en do not share a common heritage, but they do share a

common theme: both occasions symbolize the victory of good over evil with many lights – pumpkin lanterns and Diwali *diyas*.

When activities such as feasting and lighting fires occur in ceremonies, they serve deep, primal needs within the social psyche – needs that transcend cultural differences. In Autumn and Winter festivals, fires chase away darkness; in early Spring or Summer rituals, they welcome the light. Other

The Coligny calendar, a 1st-century lunar calendar, uses Roman letters and numerals along with Gaulish language, showing how as communities blend, their traditions integrate and influence one another.

festivals honour the occasions in the farming year upon which our survival depends, from ploughing to harvest. Whatever customs we celebrate, they reflect a deep-seated attachment to life-sustaining continuities.

FAREWELL AND WELCOME

Seasonal rituals give rightful symbolic importance to significant changes in the natural year, marking the passage from one phase to the next. Some events bid farewell to the old season by, for example, burning symbols or icons of last year's harvest before beginning the new harvest. Others salute the new season with actions such as, at a very basic level, wearing new clothes in Spring.

Rituals that close the old season and usher in the new create a brief symbolic "space" in the flow of time. This limbo period between old and new is full of both possibility and danger. Because it is symbolically outside ordinary time, alternative behaviour can be acted out which would otherwise be unacceptable. People wear masks or costumes to hide their identity, or indulge in cross-dressing; the normal social hierarchy becomes the subject of satire and jokes. Dead ancestors, fairies or other non-earthly beings can return to Earth. Traditions like these are particularly evident at the Celtic festivals marking the transition to Summer and Winter: Beltane (see page 54) and Samhain (see page 114).

However, all this "disruption" can be brought under control by symbolic acts of closure that restore order and guarantee the continued progression of the seasons and a regular continuity of experience. Taking down the Christmas decorations by Twelfth Night is, for example, a common closure ritual. Or sometimes a symbol of the passing season, such as the last sheaf of wheat at harvest time, is put in a safe place until next year, when it will be replaced to mark the start of a new phase in the cycle of the year.

MYTHS AND SYMBOLISM

In many cultures, the timing of a particular festival is dictated by a story or myth, often with a seasonal theme – thus, the northern European festivities of May Day, traditionally marked by the first blossoming of the hawthorn tree, are echoed in flower festivals around the world. Key points in the year are also dedicated to the celebration of particular saints or deities, and the dates for these may overlap between cultures – for example, December 25, on which Christians celebrate the birth of Christ, is also the time at which the ancient Romans celebrated the rebirth of the sun and the god Mithras. A study of the year's ceremonies around the world reveals many such fascinating correspondences.

Seasonal and Sacred Calendars

Many societies have felt that their calibration of the year offers a profound connection with the workings of the cosmos. It is hardly surprising, therefore, that ancient calendars often had a sacred status.

• • • • •

Throughout history, calendars have been drawn up by astrologers, farmers, priests and politicians to set important dates within the year. The oldest known calendar is painted on cave walls in Lascaux in the Dordogne region of France, where Cro-Magnon man appears to have recorded the phases of the moon approximately 20,000 years ago. Even before that, hunters elsewhere in Europe were making lines and holes in sticks and bones, perhaps also to mark the lunar cycle.

Five thousand years ago, in the Fertile Crescent, where the first cities were established, a calendar partitioned the year into months of 30 days, each divided into 12 sections of 2 hours, and subdivided into 30 sections of 4 minutes. A thousand or so years later, the great stone circle of Stonehenge in southern England set precise coordinates for seasonal and celestial events, including solstices and lunar eclipses. Other ancient calendars include that of the Babylonians, which had a 354-day year, and the more complex calendars of the Maya and later the Aztecs in Central America – with their vast interlocking cycles, like wheels of different sizes connected to each other by cogs.

Our own modern calendar, with its leap year every four years, was established by Pope Gregory XIII in 1582, in an attempt to regularize the timing of Easter and coordinate the lunar months with the solar year (see pages 14–15). This Gregorian calendar took a few hundred years to be fully established across Europe, but is now almost universally recognized, at least as a practical secular framework alongside the religious year.

THE CALENDAR TODAY

Our modern calendar is a complex hybrid, with a vast miscellany of historical survivals buried within it, like shards of ancient pottery within the strata of an archaeological dig. These fragments of history determine the way we think about particular times of year and the actions we perform at those times. Particular festive celebrations based on living religious beliefs will often have underlying layers of significance inherited from earlier times, or even from other belief systems. The Easter egg, for example, has a pre-Christian significance, denoting growth and renewal. This complements its use in Easter celebrations, which commemorate Christ's resurrection. Indeed, eggs are a universal symbol of rebirth, and can also be found as symbols in Judaism, Zoroastrianism and many other religions around the world.

Even where the Gregorian calendar governs the pace of daily life, and religious festivals are either observed or ignored according to cultural circumstances or individual choice, the old seasonal observances still exert a hold on our imagination. We still respond to the resonances of Imbolc, Beltane, Lammas and Samhain, the great festivals of the Celtic year; and, in the same way, we respond to the poetry of the seasons, even if we no longer feel their power so immediately.

An Aztec calendar stone, c.1400CE. In the centre is Tonatiuh, the Aztec sun god, surrounded by 20 "day signs" from the Aztec sacred calendar.

Cycles of Sun and Moon

The sun and the moon follow observable patterns across our skies, which repeat at regular intervals, and impact on our days and our tides. So it is unsurprising that the cycles of these celestial bodies are at the heart of all ancient calendars.

• • • • •

The lengthening and shortening of the days throughout the seasons are readily noticed, and the period between one full moon and the next is easily measured. These events thus form the basis of most calendars. In a religious context, sun and moon are often seen as opposing yet complementary forces, alternating in power as the seasons change.

LUNAR AND SOLAR CALENDARS

The oldest known calendars, such as the cave paintings at Lascaux (see page 12), are based on the changing appearance of the moon (*luna* in Latin). Today the only widely used calendar that is purely lunar is the Islamic one. Most calendars are lunisolar — that is, they measure the months according to

These two details of 13th-century French illuminated manuscripts show the phases of the sun (above), and the moon in relation to the sun (opposite).

the time between one full moon and the next (approximately 29.5 days), within a larger cycle based on the apparent movements of the sun as it orbits the Earth. The solar cycle can be measured by the length of the days (marking the time between the longest day of one year and the next) or by the inferred position of the sun in relation to other stars.

In a solar calendar, dates stay aligned with the seasons from one year to the next, whereas in a purely lunar calendar, they will shift from one season to another over time. However, neither lunar months nor solar years correspond in their length to an exact number of days. The time between full moons is actually 29.53 days, meaning that even if a lunar calendar alternates between 29- and 30-day months, it will still fall approximately 11 days short of the 365.242 days it takes the Earth to orbit the sun. In solar calendars, each year is approximately a quarter of a day short. These problems are generally addressed in lunar calendars by inserting an extra month approximately every fourth year to bring matters back into line, so that some years have 12 months and others 13 (as in the Hebrew and Chinese systems); and in solar calendars by inserting a surplus day every fourth (leap) year, so that three 365-

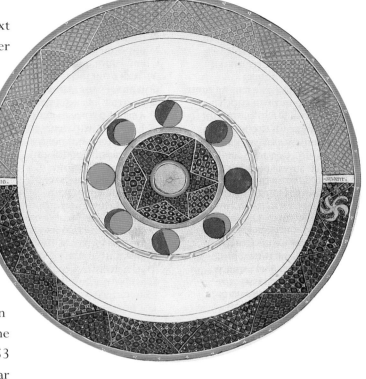

day years are followed by one of 366 days. Lunisolar calendars manage, in their hybrid way, to follow astronomical time with an acceptable accuracy.

The Gregorian calendar followed in most of the Western world today is essentially a lunisolar calendar – a modified version of an old Roman calendar which originated in its current form under Julius Caesar. This earlier calendar, known as the Julian calendar, had key details in common with our own, including a 12-month lunar cycle and the use of "leap" years.

Solstices and Equinoxes

The solstices and the equinoxes, which repeat annually, are the cornerstones of many ancient calendars.

· · · · ·

Given that nature is a cycle with no beginning or end, it may seem artificial to place fixed points around the calendar. Changes in the weather from year to year can confuse the pattern, and in any case, one season tends to merge seamlessly into another. However, there are four dates that are indisputable, as they are set by the sun. These are the longest and the shortest days (the solstices), and the days on which darkness and daylight are of equal duration (the equinoxes). These four key points are celebrated with festivals that reflect the nature of the season in which they occur.

Spring Equinox – March 21

The Spring Equinox in March marks the first balance point of the year, when night and day reach equal length. Nature bursts forth with fresh abundance. Mating spring hares and birds' eggs symbolize this time, giving us the Easter rabbits and Easter eggs of modern custom. Many of the Spring Equinox celebrations are concerned above all with resurrection – a return to life after a period of abeyance, and this is reflected in worldwide festivals of fertility, freshness and rebirth.

Summer Solstice – June 21

This is the longest day of the year, with the greatest amount of daylight and the shortest night. It has been celebrated for as long as records exist. Prehistoric monuments across the globe align with sunrise on the Summer Solstice, from Stonehenge in southern England to Macchu Picchu in Peru. The sun is at the height of its power and nature's energies are strongest. The crops are growing, so it is a time for rest and celebrations, often featuring bonfires to welcome the sun.

Autumn Equinox – September 21

The second balance point of the year falls in September, on the Autumn Equinox. For the second time in the yearly cycle, day and night are of equal length, but this time the balance tips back toward winter as the darkness begins to close in once again. Whereas the Spring Equinox celebrated the resurrection of life, the Autumn Equinox now celebrates the harvest, as the spirit of nature withdraws its energies into the earth, to rest and regenerate. Christian and Pagan harvest festivals give thanks for the sustenance provided, and wine is particularly important.

Winter Solstice – December 21

This is the shortest day of the year, when the hours of darkness are longest in relation to daylight. It marks the mid-point of Winter, when communities have traditionally drawn together to support one another, making this an important festival date in many cultures and religions. Midwinter is the "quiet time", when nature sleeps and regenerates. It appears lifeless, but after the Winter Solstice the sun begins to grow in power again. Evergreens are brought into the house to remind us of the endurance of life, and joyous festivals focus on linking communities together.

Understanding the Ancient Year

The turning points of each season, marked by the Celts with festivals celebrating the highlights of the farming year, combine with the astronomical cycle of the solstices and equinoxes, to give us what is called the "Wheel of the Year".

• • • • •

This eight-point "wheel", based on two separate cycles superimposed on each other, forms the structure of this book. First there is the march of the seasons, astronomically determined, whose highlights are the two solstices and the two equinoxes. Interwoven with this pattern is the natural cycle of the farming year, devised on the basis of experience – the best times to achieve success in various agricultural tasks, from arable farming to animal husbandry. The farming year has four major celebrations, which the Celts associated with key agricultural events. Together, the two cycles make up the "Wheel of the Year".

THE CELTIC FESTIVALS

Of the four major Celtic festivals, the two most important are the "fire festivals" – Beltane (meaning "bright fire"), which takes place on May 1 and celebrates the end of Winter; and Samhain (pronounced "Saow-in"), on October 31, which marks the end of Summer. Samhain initiates the first half of the year, which the Celts knew as the "dark" time. Beltane marks the beginning of the second, "light" half of the year. Bonfires were lit for both festivals on the eve of the day itself, and the Celts drove their livestock between these fires to burn off any parasites and therefore prevent disease.

The other two festivals are Imbolc, which falls at the beginning of February, and Lammas (also known as Lughnasadh; pronounced "Loo-nasa") at the beginning of August. Imbolc is associated with the birth of young animals, lactation and the Celtic goddess Brighid; while Lammas marks the start of the harvest. The term Lughnasadh refers to the feast of the god Lugh.

WINTER *Yule*

AUTUMN TURNS TO WINTER *Samhain*

WINTER TURNS TO SPRING *Imbolc*

AUTUMN *Mabon*

SPRING *Ostara*

SUMMER TURNS TO AUTUMN *Lammas*

SPRING TURNS TO SUMMER *Beltane*

SUMMER *Litha*

THE WHEEL OF THE YEAR

The "Wheel of the Year" (see right) provides the basic eight-part structure by which this book is organized. Each chapter focuses on the traditions, beliefs and festivals associated with the time of year to which it relates: four marking the turning of one season into another (Imbolc, Beltane, Lammas and Samhain), and the other four marking the high point of each season (Ostara, Litha, Mabon and Yule). The Celts are given prominence within this structure, as their festivals are so richly evocative and deep-rooted within the European, and consequently the colonial American, tradition; while the solstices and equinoxes are universal. And the impact of Christian belief and ceremony on the Wheel is one of the leitmotifs of this book.

Ostara, Litha and Mabon

Unlike Imbolc, Beltane, Lammas, Samhain and Yule, which have their origins in ancient Celtic tradition, the use of Ostara, Litha and Mabon as terms to denote Spring, Midsummer and the Autumn Equinox owes a debt to modern Paganism. Ostara was identified by the Venerable Bede, an 8th-century Christian writer who linked an otherwise unknown Saxon goddess called Eostre to a Spring festival called Ostara in his examination of the Anglo-Saxon calendar, *De Tempore Rationum* (On the Reckoning of Time).

"Early Litha" as a name for June, and "Late Litha" for July, are terms recorded in the same source. Midsummer has therefore come to be known as Litha, from an Anglo-Saxon word which translates as "calm", reflecting the restful pause in the farming year during this period. The creation of the term Litha is sometimes erroneously attributed to J.R.R. Tolkien, who brought it into popular usage in his *Lord of the Rings* novels.

Mabon is derived from the Welsh folkloric figure Mabon vab Modron. He was known as Maponus to the Romans and was associated with hunting, poetry and music. The use of the term Mabon for the Autumn Equinox began in the mid-20th century.

THE TURNING WHEEL
As the Wheel of the Year turns, ceremonies with links to myth, belief, history, nature and farming are celebrated throughout the world.

WINTER TURNS TO SPRING
Imbolc

WINTER
Yule

SPRING
Ostara

FEBRUARY

MARCH

JANUARY

APRIL

SPRING TURNS TO SUMMER
Beltane

DECEMBER

MAY

AUTUMN TURNS TO WINTER
Samhain

NOVEMBER

JUNE

OCTOBER

JULY

AUTUMN
Mabon

SUMMER
Litha

SEPTEMBER

AUGUST

SUMMER TURNS TO AUTUMN
Lammas

• **WINTER TURNS TO SPRING:** *Ceremonies celebrate newness — the birth of new lambs, and the emergence of shoots and early blossoms.*

• **SPRING:** *People celebrate burgeoning fertility, rebirth and the balance of opposing forces at the equinox.*

• **SPRING TURNS TO SUMMER:** *Festivities centre on traditions and deities associated with the flourishing of nature.*

• **SUMMER:** *The regenerating power of the sun is celebrated, along with fertility and ripening in the natural world.*

• **SUMMER TURNS TO AUTUMN:** *The gods and goddesses responsible for the harvest are propitiated with grain festivities.*

• **AUTUMN:** *Celebrations focus on the harvested crops, particularly wine, and on balance and justice.*

• **AUTUMN TURNS TO WINTER:** *Bonfires light up the short, dark nights as people honour the dead and mark the end of harvest.*

• **WINTER:** *Communities gather together to reflect on the past year and to celebrate the return of the light.*

 Winter
TURNS TO
Spring

February 1 – March 20

"No matter how long the Winter,
Spring is sure to follow."

PROVERB IN VARIOUS TRADITIONS

• • • • •

Emergence 24
First Flowers 26
Brighid, the Bright One 28
Candlemas 30
Chinese New Year 32
Groundhog Day 33
Love Festivals 34

Emergence

As flowers and animals begin to flourish, the onset of Spring and the renewal of life are a universal tonic in temperate climes — a cause for celebration in many ancient cultures.

• • • • •

The first of the four great Celtic festivals is Imbolc, which falls at the beginning of February. Now begins the time of awakening as the daylight hours grow noticeably longer. February has always been an important month for agricultural communities. The first lambs are born in the fields, ewes begin to lactate (the Celtic name Imbolc means "lactation"), and fresh milk and dairy products once again become available. In previous centuries, this could have meant the difference between life and death, particularly for children and the elderly. In Pagan tradition, fresh milk is poured onto the ground as a tribute to Mother Earth and to ritually request fertility for the coming season.

"Good Fortune in!"

On February 3 in Japan, at the Shinto festival of Setsubun-sai, people celebrate the change of seasons and the coming of spring with shouts of "Devils out, Good Fortune in!". They throw roasted soy beans (*mame*) over the thresholds of Shinto temples, through the doors of their houses or inside their homes to purify these spaces and to chase away evil spirits. Afterwards, each person picks up and eats the number of beans corresponding to their age, plus one to guarantee good luck in the coming year.

THE TURNING WHEEL

Ceremonies in early Spring celebrate newness — the birth of new lambs, the re-emergence of green shoots and the blossoming of the earliest Spring flowers.

• **IMBOLC**
February 1: *Celtic festival celebrating the birth of the first lambs*

• **CANDLEMAS**
February 1: *Christian commemoration of the presentation of Jesus Christ in the Temple at Jerusalem*

• **FEAST OF BRIGHID/ST BRIDE**
February 1: *Overlapping Celtic and Christian celebration of a saint associated with light and the protection of livestock*

• **VALENTINE'S DAY**
February 14: *Worldwide event in honour of romantic love*

• **GROUNDHOG DAY**
February 2: *North American ritual in which a groundhog "predicts" the Spring weather*

WINTER TURNS TO SPRING
Imbolc

FEBRUARY MARCH

Feast of Imbolc

WINTER
Yule

SPRING
Ostara

AUTUMN TURNS TO WINTER
Samhain

SPRING TURNS TO SUMMER
Beltane

AUTUMN
Mabon

SUMMER
Litha

SUMMER TURNS TO AUTUMN
Lammas

First Flowers

The pure white snowdrop first appears on the ground in early Spring, heralding the return of life — a symbol of hope amid the lingering frosts.

• • • • •

Acommon icon of early Spring, and a sacred plant of the season in both Pagan and Christian tradition, is the snowdrop. The flower's latin name is *Galanthus nivalis*, meaning "milk flower of the snow" – perhaps because snowdrops appear at the same time as the first milk of lactating ewes. These delicate flowers start to bloom at the beginning of February, as reflected in this couplet from an early 16th-century English church calendar of flowers:

The snowdrop, in purest white array,
First rears her head on
Candlemas day.

In some churches in England and Ireland, the image of the Virgin Mary is taken down on February 2 – Candlemas (see pages 30–31) – and snowdrops are spread in its place. Other names for the plant are the Fair Maid of February, Candlemas Bells and Mary's Tapers. Its appearance marks the end of Winter with a delicately beautiful promise.

FOLK TALES

A tale from German folklore explains the snowdrop's early blossoming. When God created snow, he told it to go to the flowers and ask them to give it some of their colour. Only the little snowdrop agreed, and as a reward, God made snowdrops the first flowers to bloom.

In Christian legend, snowdrops were created by an angel to console Adam and Eve after their exile from the garden of Eden. He blew upon falling snowflakes and, as they touched the ground, snowdrops emerged where they fell, to reassure Adam and Eve that Spring would come, despite their shameful transgression.

"*Bread feeds the body, indeed,*
but flowers feed also the soul . . ."
THE KORAN

Brighid, the Bright One

Both Celtic goddess and Christian saint, Brighid, or Brigid, is celebrated on February 1. She presides over fertility and the protection of the hearth and livestock.

• • • • •

The Celts saw Imbolc as a time of purification, in preparation for the coming year. They celebrated the festival by lighting fires to honour Brighid, whose name derives from an Irish epithet, *Brid*, meaning "bright one". In Scotland, Brighid took over the role previously filled by Cailleach Bheur, a supernatural woman supposedly older than the oldest animals. Brighid also had a warlike British counterpart in Brigantia, goddess of the Brigantes tribe of Yorkshire, better known today as Britannia. Brighid later took on a Christian aspect as St Brigid (also known as St Bride, and sometimes Mary of the Gael). The

A 15th-century illustration of St Bride of Kildare, from an English illuminated manuscript.

patron saint of Ireland, she was second only to St Patrick in importance. The Christian St Brigid was a real person who lived in Ireland from the mid-5th century until 525CE, her mother supposedly being a Christian Pictish slave whom St Patrick had baptized. Brigid founded a community of nuns and monks at Kildare, replacing an earlier Pagan sanctuary in which a sacred flame was kept burning.

BRINGER OF LUCK

The importance of milk at this time of year is echoed in a legend of St Brigid. As a girl she was unable to eat food prepared by her Druid stepfather, until he gave her the milk of a cow milked by a Christian woman. This blending of Celtic myth and Christian folktale, to create a story in which Christianity replaces Paganism, is characteristic of the way in which the early Church transformed many existing beliefs.

St Brigid was also venerated as the midwife of the Virgin Mary, who wrapped the baby Jesus in swaddling clothes. In Ireland, on the night of the feast in her honour, February 1, people left a piece of cloth outside their house; and if it was marked the next day, they believed that St Brigid had passed by and blessed them with good luck.

BRIGID'S CROSS

In another story, St Brigid washed her clothes and hung them on a sunbeam, which then miraculously solidified and shone warmly until her clothes were dry.

A lucky charm associated with Imbolc, Brigid's Cross (left) resembles the sun with four sunbeams. Such crosses were made in ancient Ireland and are still fashioned today by weaving rushes, straw or even strips of paper together. Hanging a Brigid's cross over your door protects, purifies and brings good fortune to the home.

The Triple Goddess

Brighid is a "triune" goddess, meaning that she is simultaneously one and three. In modern Paganism, she is the maiden aspect of a Celtic "Triple Goddess", a single goddess with three aspects or faces: maiden, a young girl often shown carrying the flowers of spring; mother, often portrayed as a pregnant woman and associated with the harvest and Lammas (see page 84); and crone, an old woman who has become the traditional Hallowe'en witch.

The Triple Goddess represents the cycle of life and also the continuous regeneration of nature, as her three ages can be equated to the seasons of Spring (maiden), Summer (mother) and Autumn (crone). Winter represents death. During early Spring, the goddess is in her maiden aspect: a young girl who is waking up to womanhood just as nature begins its fertility cycle. The maiden is celebrated in many forms, including Brighid and the Virgin Mary.

Candlemas

In the modern Church calendar, Candlemas — which takes place on February 2, the day after Imbolc — commemorates the purification of the Virgin Mary in the Temple of Jerusalem, 40 days after the birth of Christ.

• • • • •

In churches today at Candlemas, the priest blesses all the candles that will be used in that church throughout the year. Some of them are then distributed to the congregation, lighted and carried in a solemn procession. Traditionally, members of the congregation will also have brought their own candles to the church to be blessed for use during the year. Candles are still sometimes displayed in the windows of houses on this day. The Emperor Justinian introduced Candlemas to the Eastern Church in 542. In the 8th century the Venerable Bede mentioned the occasion in his *Ecclesiastical History of England*.

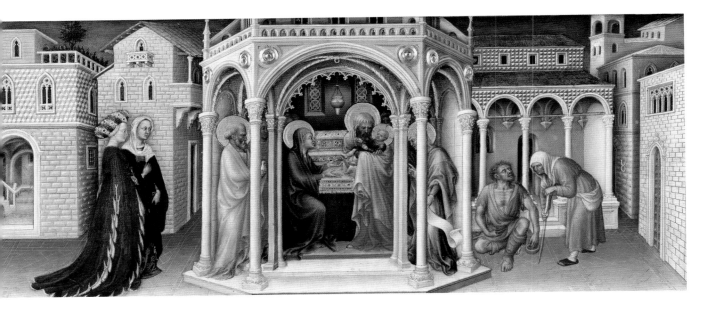

Lent

The period of Lent, the 40 days preceding Easter Sunday and the most important period of fasting in the Judeo-Christian world, recalls Jesus' period of abstinence as he wandered in the wilderness, where he experienced visions and was tempted by the Devil. In Western Christianity, Easter takes place on the first Sunday after the full moon following the Spring Equinox (which places it between late March and late April), and so Shrove Tuesday, the onset of Lent, similarly moves back and forth, between mid-February and mid-March. Lent is a period of austerity, when certain foods are prohibited, traditionally including eggs and alcohol. Pancakes were traditionally made on Shrove Tuesday to use up many of the prohibited foodstuffs left in the home, and pancake-making remains an important feature of this day, although few now observe the dietary restrictions that used to follow.

In Biblical times, Jewish women were permitted to return to the Temple 40 days after the birth of a boy (and 80 days after the birth of a girl). During the service, the mother would be symbolically purified of sin, and the child would be presented to the congregation. As the birth of Christ is fixed at December 25 in the Christian calendar, his mother Mary's return to the Temple would have taken place on February 2.

This panel from a 15th-century altarpiece shows Jesus being presented in the Temple. Simeon holds the baby Jesus, while his mother, Mary, stands to their right.

Jesus' conception and birth were held to be miraculous, and his special status was recognized when he was still an infant. According to the Gospel of Luke, when the baby Jesus was presented at the Temple, he was met by Simeon and Anna. Simeon took the baby boy into his arms, and prophesied that the child would become "a light for revelation … and for glory", bringing light into the world in the same way that a candle brings light to the darkness.

The procession that takes place in churches at Candlemas symbolizes Christ's entry into the Temple.

Chinese New Year

Good fortune, longevity, wealth and happiness are all prayed for at Chinese New Year. Also known as the Spring Festival, this event falls on the first day of the first month of the Chinese lunar calendar, between late January and mid-February.

• • • • •

The lavish festivities of Chinese New Year last two weeks. It is a time to visit friends and family, and hold reunions and parties. Delicious traditional foods are a key feature of these gatherings, particularly dumplings (*jiaozi*). Ingredients are often chosen because of the auspicious sound of their name – thus, fish (*yú*) is included because the word *yú* sounds similar to the word for "surplus" – so that eating fish is thought to encourage abundance in the coming year.

This is a time when the lucky colour red appears everywhere – for example, children receive small red packets of money decorated with gold characters to signify wealth. Families also decorate the outsides of their homes with paper cut-outs of phrases that speak of positive values, such as joy or good fortune. The celebrations end with the Lantern festival at full moon on the fifteenth day, which is marked with fireworks, many lanterns and often processions involving dancing lion and dragon puppets.

Huge, brightly coloured festive lanterns process through a Hong Kong street at New Year. Dragons are considered auspicious in Chinese tradition.

Groundhog Day

According to legend, the weather on Candlemas (February 2) dictates the weather for the remaining weeks of Winter. This belief is mirrored in the modern ritual of Groundhog Day observed in Pennsylvania, USA.

• • • • •

An old English folk tradition states that if the weather on Candlemas is fair, the remaining weeks of Winter (until March 21, the Spring Equinox) will be cold and stormy. However, if the weather is bad on Candlemas, the rest of the Winter will be mild. This is expressed in the verse:

> *If Candlemas be fair and bright*
> *Winter has another flight.*
> *If Candlemas brings clouds and rain*
> *Winter will not come again.*

WEATHER WISE

As January turns to February, the North American groundhog awakens from hibernation and emerges from its burrow. According to legend, if it sees its own shadow, showing that the sun is shining, it retreats underground and stays there for another six weeks, as this means that Winter is far from over. If clouds obliterate the shadow, the weeks ahead will be mild, so the creature emerges from its home and remains outside for the rest of the year.

Pennsylvanian Dutch settlers brought the tradition of Groundhog Day to the USA in the 18th century (the animal used was orginally a dachs, a relation of the European badger). The "official" groundhog now charged with weather prediction lives in Punxsutawney, Pennsylvania, where on the morning of February 2 each year he is taken out of his den by his top-hatted keepers, the Groundhog Club, and is believed to whisper his forecast to the club's president.

The original version of the legend recalls the ancient Greek belief that an animal's shadow was its soul, which had been darkened by the year's sins. Hibernation was a time of spiritual renewal. Any animal that saw its own shadow would know that it needed to hibernate longer in order for the shadow to be expunged by further purification.

Love Festivals

Wintry weather persists and most birds are not yet ready to sing and display, but early Spring has a welcome theme: courtship and the celebration of love.

• • • • •

During the Middle Ages, there was a common belief in England and France that birds started to look for a mate on February 14. On this day, many countries around the world celebrate our most familiar love festival: Valentine's Day. The tradition is recorded as far back as Chaucer, who refers to "Seynt Valentyne's day" in his long poem, *Parlement of Foules (c.1382)*.

LUPERCALIA

Valentine's Day has its origins in the Roman festival of Lupercalia, observed on February 15, in the last month of the Roman year. Lupercalia celebrated the coming of Spring and honoured the Roman god Faunus, who protected shepherds and their flocks, as well as (later) Romulus and Remus, the mythical founders of Rome who were raised by a she-wolf (*lupa* in Latin). Lupercalia became a celebration to guarantee the fertility of flocks, fields and people, and it was also a love festival.

To begin the proceedings, members of the Luperci, an order of priests, would gather at the sacred cave where the infants Romulus and Remus were believed to have been raised. The priests would sacrifice a goat for fertility and a dog for purification. The goat's hide was then cut into strips, dipped into the sacrificial blood and taken to the streets. Not only fields of crops but also women were then touched with these hides, as it was believed the strips would make them more fertile in the coming year. Later in the day, according to legend, all the young women in the city would place their names in a large urn, and bachelor men would draw one out, thereby choosing a partner for the remainder of the celebrations. Lupercalia transformed and spread as the Roman Empire grew.

An English Valentine's token from the Victorian era. The smaller heart contains a message which reads: "Accept this Loving Heart of Mine."

VALENTINE'S DAY

According to legend, Emperor Claudius II (ruled 268–270CE) banned young men from marriage as he believed it made soldiers reluctant to leave on the long campaigns vital to the maintenance of the Roman Empire. St Valentine was a Christian priest sympathetic to the desires of young lovers, who married many in secret. Eventually, he was captured and put to death on February 14, 269CE. While awaiting his execution he passed a final message to the blind daughter of his jailor Asterius, with whom he had become friends: this was the first Valentine's card.

During the Middle Ages, Valentine's messages became popular in Europe. Love notes were spoken, sung, or written down and passed between lovers. For example, in 1415 the young French nobleman, Charles, Duke of Orleans, sent a love poem to his wife while being held prisoner in the Tower of London. Women entered their names in Valentine's lotteries, and the man who chose a particular woman wore her name on his sleeve (hence the phrase "wearing one's heart on one's sleeve"), and it was his duty to protect her for a year.

Handmade paper Valentines were already common in England during the 16th century. Symbols such as hearts were often used instead of signing one's name – often because the sender was illiterate.

In Japan, women buy chocolates for men on Valentine's Day: *kiri-choco*, for friends and family, or *hon-mei*, for husbands or lovers. A month later, on White Day, the men reciprocate.

Spring

March 21 – April 30

"Spring has returned. The Earth is like a child that knows poems."

RAINER MARIA RILKE (1875–1926)

• • • • •

Spring Equinox 38
New Beginnings 40
The Roots of Modern Easter 42
Festivals of Colour, Love and Motherhood 46
Spring Storms and the Wind Flower 48
Resurrected Gods 50

Spring Equinox

The Spring Equinox falls on March 20, 21 or 22 in the northern hemisphere. It is the first of the year's two balance points, at which day and night each lasts for exactly 12 hours.

• • • • •

The Latin word *equinox* means "equal night" – the day and the night at this time are of equal length all over the planet. After the Spring Equinox, the period of daylight increases, gradually becoming longer in relation to the hours of night until a grand climax is reached at the Summer Solstice, the longest day.

Darkness continues to yield to light as the Earth shrugs off the sleep of winter completely. Plants and trees unfurl their leaves, and flowers bud. Another name for March 21 is the Vernal Equinox, from the Latin *vernare*, to bloom, and this is reflected in the names of many spring-flowering plants, such as *Lathyrus vernus*, the sweet pea.

New life and fresh beginnings are celebrated. Thus ensues the true spring, the relief of mild weather – and in the valleys (it is to be hoped) the last of the frosts.

Trumpets of the Sun

Many flowers associated with this time of year, such as daffodils, have bright yellow blooms, heralding the triumph of the sun. The yellow centre of the daisy, in particular, has associations in Celtic tradition not only with the sun, but also with the yolk of the eggs that are first laid at this time of year. The name "daisy" comes from "day's eye": like a human eye, the flower is closed tightly at night and open during the daytime.

THE TURNING WHEEL
Ceremonies taking place around the Spring Equinox focus on burgeoning fertility and rebirth.

• **EASTER**
Moveable: *The most important festival in the Christian calendar, commemorating Jesus Christ's resurrection*

• **NORUZ**
March 21: *New Year in the Baha'i faith, which has its roots in Zoroastrian tradition*

Spring Equinox (earliest point at which Easter can fall)

SPRING
Ostara

MARCH

APRIL

• **OSTARA**
March 21: *Pagan festival celebrating Eostre, the goddess of Spring*

WINTER TURNS TO SPRING
Imbolc

WINTER
Yule

AUTUMN TURNS TO WINTER
Samhain

SPRING TURNS TO SUMMER
Beltane

Latest point at which Easter can fall

AUTUMN
Mabon

SUMMER
Litha

SUMMER TURNS TO AUTUMN
Lammas

• **HOLI**
Moveable: *Hindu "festival of colour", marked with joyful festivities, including street parties*

• **MOTHER'S DAY**
Moveable:
Celebration of motherhood, derived from the Roman festival of Matronalia

• **FEAST OF THE ANNUNCIATION**
March 25: *Christian festival celebrating the Immaculate Conception*

New Beginnings

March 21 is the start of the New Year in several cultures; it is also the beginning of the astrological year. Festivals and rituals rejoice in the progression from promise to actuality: Winter is not on its last legs, it is well and truly defeated.

• • • • •

The Achaemenians, a dynasty of kings who ruled Persia from 648 to 330 BCE, celebrated the Spring Equinox at their great city of Persepolis with the festival of Noruz. Stone carvings from the period depict subjects, governors and ambassadors carrying gifts to present to the Persian king.

Noruz, which translates as "new day", is a celebration of hope and renewal which is still observed in Turkey, Pakistan, Iran and Afghanistan. It is rooted in Zoroastrianism, the major religion in ancient Persia (Iran) until the arrival of Islam in the 7th century. Today, Noruz is the most cherished festival in the Iranian calendar, where it is celebrated over a period of 13 days.

RED WEDNESDAY AND FIROUZ

The month of Farvardin (the first month of the Iranian calendar) is named for the Fravashis, guardian spirits who return to the world in the last ten days of each year. Feasts and street parties take place throughout Iran over this time. Iranians take ritual cleansing baths on the first day and wear new clothes to symbolize the fresh start of a new year. A festival called *Chahar-Shanbeh Suri* ("the Eve of Red Wednesday") falls on the last Wednesday before Noruz begins. People purify their homes with a thorough spring-cleaning, and leap over fires lit on their rooftops at night, for luck and to welcome back the Fravashis.

In the days before Noruz, performers appear dressed as Haji Firouz, a troubadour clothed in bright red or green who announces the coming of the New Year. These performers dance and sing funny songs accompanied by a small percussion instrument similar to a tambourine, called a *dayereh zangy*. As well as being a spirit protector of the dead, Haji Firouz strove to make people laugh, presaging their good humour for the year ahead.

A RAM IN THE ZODIAC

The astrological year also begins on March 21, the first day of Aries. This, the first sign of the Zodiac, is ruled by the planet Mars, and thus is associated with both the Greek and Roman gods of war (Ares and Mars). The Roman god Mars was also an agricultural deity, who represented fertility, new growth and Spring. He was worshipped as a healing god by the Celts, as he protected faithful devotees from disease.

A procession of gift bearers advances up one of the magnificent ceremonial staircases at Persepolis, Iran. Darius I began construction of Persepolis in c.509BCE.

The designation of Aries as the Ram goes back to Mesopotamia in the third millennium BCE. In Greek myth, this constellation represents the Golden Fleece shorn from a magical flying ram – the prize sought by Jason, the great Greek voyager-hero, who sailed to find it in his ship, the *Argo*.

The Roots of Modern Easter

Easter celebrations in Christian countries are explicitly related to Christ's sacrifice. However, many traditions associated with Easter have their origins outside Christianity, in various forms of rejoicing for the return of Spring.

• • • • •

The date of Easter is not fixed: it falls on the first Sunday following the full moon either on or after the Spring Equinox (March 21 in ecclesiastical calendars). However, in Orthodox Christianity, the date of Easter is determined by the date of Passover – the Last Supper shared by Jesus and his disciples before the Crucifixion is thought to have been a *seder* (the ritual meal eaten at Passover).

Passover, which marks the exodus of the Israelites from Egypt, is called *Pesach* in Hebrew. In parts of Europe the name for the Christian festival held at this time derives from Pesach: the French for Easter is *Pâques*, the Spanish, *Pascua*, and the Dutch, *Pasen*.

EOSTRE AND THE EGG

Pagan traditions give us the English name Easter, which comes from the word Eostre.

The Anglo-Saxons' word for March was *Estor-monath* (the month of openings). According to an account by the Venerable Bede (see page 20), *Estor-monath* was named in honour of the Saxon goddess of the dawn, Eostre. Nothing definite is known about this goddess, but rituals related to her (and to Easter, by association) focus on new beginnings, symbolized by the Easter egg, and fertility, which is symbolized by the hare (or Easter bunny).

The egg's oval shape represents the eternal cycle of the seasons. In the modern Pagan celebration of Ostara, the egg represents the cosmic egg of creation and rebirth. In Pagan tradition, the egg's yolk symbolizes the sun-god, and the egg-white and pale shell represent the maiden goddess: their sacred marriage is said to have occurred at the Spring Equinox.

In ancient agricultural societies, eggs provided a vital source of nutrition. By mid-March, food stores from the previous year would have been running low. The first eggs of the year, laid by domesticated fowl or foraged from the nests of wild birds, added much-needed nutrients to people's diet. The custom of hunting for Easter eggs derives from the need to forage for wild birds' eggs at this time of year.

MAD MARCH HARES

The Spring Equinox is also the time when seeds are sown for the Autumn harvest, and nature's fertility is therefore both prayed for and celebrated. The March Hare was a widely recognized fertility symbol in medieval Europe. The majority of northern European species of hare are nocturnal for most of the year, but from March 1 they are in season and need to mate, so appear during the day. In addition, female hares can conceive a second litter of

Exchanging Eggs

A charming legend tells how the Saxon goddess Eostre found a wounded bird and transformed it into a hare, so that it could survive the Winter. The hare found that it could lay eggs, so it decorated these each Spring and left them as an offering to the goddess. Among the traditions associated with Noruz (see pages 40–41), Iranians give gifts of eggs dyed red to mark the new year's first day. Ancient Egyptians, Greeks and Romans also celebrated spring with coloured eggs. Traditionally, eggs were dyed red to symbolize Christ's blood, and red is also associated with fertility and rebirth. The Russian tsars Alexander III and Nicholas II gave their wives exquisite enamelled Fabergé eggs at Easter – a custom which became fashionable among aristocrats and royalty in early modern Europe.

offspring while still pregnant with the first. Unreceptive females "box" persistent males to discourage them, and the rejected males then become frustrated and behave erratically. This behaviour led to the English phrases "mad as a March Hare" and "hare-brained". The first use of "mad as a March Hare" appeared in 1529, in Sir Thomas More's ecclesiastical pamphlet, *The supplycacyon of soulys*: "As mad not as a march hare, but as a madde dogge." The phrase became immortalized thanks to the appearance of an eccentric March Hare alongside the Mad Hatter in Lewis Carroll's *Alice in Wonderland*.

The modern legend of the Easter Bunny, which has its basis in the March Hare traditions, originated in Germany: it is mentioned in 16th-century writings. German settlers took the traditions with them to 17th-century America, where children would leave out nests made of grass, as well as their Easter bonnets and caps, to be filled with treats by the Easter Bunny – but could expect success only if they'd been good.

Another animal sacred to Spring is the snake, which emerges from Winter hibernation to bask in Spring sunshine. All species shed their skin several times, a process symbolic of healing and renewal.

EASTER LILIES AND LADY DAY

Pure white lilies often decorate church altars at Easter to symbolize the Annunciation and the Immaculate Conception. The feast of the Annunciation, Lady Day, is on March 25 – exactly nine months before December 25, and so, according to the Christian calendar, the day that the archangel Gabriel appeared to Mary. Paintings of the Annunciation often show Gabriel handing Mary lilies.

Hares leap through the fields in this 15th-century French manuscript. The symbolism of the Easter Bunny is related to the erratic behaviour of hares in Spring.

"*Earth, teach me regeneration,*
as the seed which rises in the Spring."

MODERN UTE PRAYER

Festivals of Colour, Love and Motherhood

This fertile period of the year is marked with energetic communal events which often have an aspect of sensuality. Other celebrations honour and bless women, particularly mothers.

• • • • •

The Hindu religion celebrates the arrival of Spring with a joyous, licentious festival: Holi, the "Festival of Colour". At Holi, people shower each other with coloured powders, water and flower petals at vibrant, boisterous street parties. Caste, age and gender barriers are set aside, which gives opportunities for mischievous pranks, flirting and romance. The sensual aspects of Holi are said to recall the passionate love of the god Krishna and Radha, his favourite among the *gopis* (milkmaids) who raised him.

Another legend associated with Holi tells of an arrogant king, Hiranyakashyapu, who declared himself to be a god. His son Prahlad, a devotee of Vishnu, the Supreme Being, refused to worship him, and the king ordered Prahlad's death – he was to be held in a fire by his aunt Holika, who was immune from burning. However, the flames did not harm Prahlad, while Holika was incinerated. Bonfires are lit the night before the Holi festival to remember this triumph of good over evil.

On the new moon in April, the ancient Romans celebrated Veneralia, which honoured Venus Verticordia ("Changer of Hearts") and also Fortuna Virilis ("Bold Fortune"), to whom women prayed for success in love. During the Veneralia festivities, all classes of women entered the men's public baths. They stripped naked, donned wreaths of myrtle leaves, drank a potion made of milk, honey and powdered poppies, and offered incense and prayers to the goddesses. In his work *Fasti*, the poet Ovid advised women that Fortuna Virilis,

Krishna and his gopis (milkmaids) celebrate Holi with music, drumming and the traditional showers of coloured powder in this 18th-century Indian manuscript.

properly appeased, would blind men to a woman's physical imperfections.

CELEBRATING MOTHERHOOD

Matronalia, the "Festival of Women", was celebrated on March 1 in ancient Rome, in honour of Juno Luciana, the goddess of women, marriage and childbirth. Luciana derives from the Latin word *lux*, meaning "light" – this goddess oversaw birth and the first light that a baby sees. On this day, men gave their lovers and wives gifts and prayed for their health. Roman wives usually wore their hair in tight braids, but pregnant women were permitted to loosen their hair at Matronalia: with Juno's blessing, this would bring an easy delivery.

Mother's Day originated in Europe during the Middle Ages. On the fourth Sunday in Lent, people living away from their home parish would return to visit their "mother" church, which led naturally to family gatherings and reunions. The custom of giving flowers arose because servants were permitted to pick a posy of flowers from their employers' gardens. Eventually, domestic servants and apprentices were officially given this Sunday off to visit their mother and family.

In the USA, Mother's Day falls not in Lent, as it does in the UK, but on the second Sunday in May. It particularly commemorates the humanitarian work carried out by mothers during and after the American Civil War.

Spring Storms and the Wind Flower

The unpredictable showers and winds of early Spring have given rise to several beliefs associated with gods of weather.

• • • • •

An old British folk rhyme reflects the weather that predominates in Spring:

*March winds and April showers
Bring forth May flowers.*

This echoes the Pagan belief that each period in the turning year has its purpose. The abundant rain may be inconvenient, but it will water the growing crops; while the strong winds will carry seeds and pollen to fertilize plants, trees and flowers.

THE SEA MITHER

In the lore of the Orkney Islands in the far north of Scotland, which combines elements of Celtic and Nordic myth, a benign Summer spirit called the Sea Mither returns in Spring. She warms the oceans and calms the Spring storms that spell danger for local fishermen. Her enemy is Teran, spirit of Winter, whose grating voice causes gales and crashing waves. The Mither's return is heralded by the *Voye Tullye* ("Spring Struggle") against Teran, which manifests itself as vicious storms. Each year the Mither is said to bind Teran at the bottom of the sea, where he remains helpless until the Autumn Equinox.

THE WIND FLOWER

The wood anemone (*Anemone nemrosa*) blooms around the time of the Spring Equinox in Europe, Asia and the Middle East. In Greek legend, *anemos* (the wind) sends the anemones in the Spring to herald his arrival – they open only when the March winds begin to blow. This gives the anemone its folkloric name of "wind flower".

A Spring carpet of anemones blooms in a Swedish woodland. According to one British folktale, picking an anemone will cause a thunderstorm.

Resurrected Gods

The theme of resurrection, so important at Christian Easter, is also apparent in Spring celebrations connected with youthful gods of light and vegetation.

• • • • •

Nature gods such as Attis, a young male deity who appears in Greek, Roman and Phrygian mythology, died at the time of the harvest in Autumn, and were reborn at the Spring Equinox. Attis was the consort of Cybele, the "Great Mother of the Gods", and at the festival dedicated to him on the Spring Equinox, their myth was re-enacted as a mystery drama. In this myth, Cybele became infatuated with a young shepherd, Attis. As he was about to be married, she induced madness in him, and he killed

Mithras and Christ

Devotees of Mithras believed that the soul descended to Earth when a person was born. At death, that person's soul was fought over by the powers of light and darkness. Christianity and Christian ritual are similarly concerned with the journey of the human soul to salvation or damnation. Mithras, like Christ, intervened for his followers, helping them to enter heaven, the realm of light. As well as this emphasis on salvation, and the Spring Equinox associations with death and resurrection, Mithras was also miraculously born on December 25 — his birth coincided with the birth of the sun at the Winter Solstice. Followers of Mithras consumed bread and water (representing the body and blood of the bull, see opposite) at communal meals and, like Jesus, Mithras was resurrected in Spring.

himself. Cybele's guilt was so great that she persuaded Zeus to restore Attis to life and make his body immune to age or disease.

Also reborn at the Spring Equinox was the god Mithras. In pre-Zoroastrian Persia, he was known as Mithra, associated with light and the changing seasons, and celebrated at the festival of Noruz (see pages 40–41). He became Mithras in ancient Rome, where he was particularly popular among the military. Symbols of Mithras were taken into underground temples during Autumn rites, and brought out again at the Spring Equinox, symbolically resurrecting the god.

The Spring theme of new life was central to Mithraic mythology. In a key episode, the sun ordered Mithras to sacrifice a white bull. He did so reluctantly, and is often depicted turning

Mithras is shown sacrificing a bull in this 2nd-century Roman sculpture.

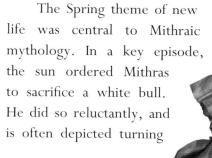

his head away from his knife. But at the moment of sacrifice, a miracle occurred: the bull's body transformed into the moon, and Mithras's cloak became the night sky. Plants and trees grew from the bull's blood, and the first ears of grain sprang from his tail.

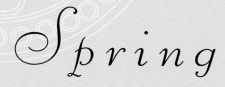

Spring

TURNS TO

Summer

May 1 – June 20

*"The month of May was come, when
every lusty heart beginneth to blossom . . ."*

SIR THOMAS MALORY (*c.*1405–1471)

• • • • •

May Day 54
A Blanket of Flowers 56
Banishing the Darkness 58
Hawthorn: the Fairy Tree 60
Horned Gods and May Games 62
The Green Man 64

May Day

In Celtic tradition, the festival of Beltane on May 1 marks the mid-point between Spring and Summer, and opens the "light half" of the Celtic year.

• • • • •

Maia, the Greco-Roman goddess of the springtime, gives us the modern English word "May". Events are held to mark the flowering of trees and plants all across the world, such as Hanami in Japan, Santa Cruz in Spain and Lei (Garland) Day in Hawaii, as well as the modern European May Day. They all celebrate the seasonal themes of brightness, blossoming and new life, as well as the arrival of Summer.

In the Gaelic languages of Ireland, Scotland and the Isle of Man, "Bealtaine" still designates May 1. Beltane (to use the Anglicized spelling) means "Bright Fire" in Celtic: bonfires were central to this festival. At Beltane, the ancient Celts released the cattle that had survived the Winter back into the fields, driving the animals between fires to purify them – with the additional effect of protecting them from parasitic diseases.

The Shining One

Roman soldiers in Celtic Europe reported seeing visions of a shining god before they went into battle. This was Belenus, a deity linked to Beltane, whose name means "shining one". In a temple dedicated to him in Burgundy, devotees left small clay horses and swaddled infants, invoking the god's protection for new life and livestock. Belenus was also believed to have healing powers, evoking the purifying effects of the Beltane fires.

THE TURNING WHEEL

Late spring and early summer festivities centre on traditions and deities associated with the blossoming of nature, and include glorious flower festivals.

WINTER TURNS TO SPRING
Imbolc

WINTER
Yule

SPRING
Ostara

AUTUMN TURNS TO WINTER
Samhain

Feast of Beltane

SPRING TURNS TO SUMMER
Beltane

MAY

JUNE

AUTUMN
Mabon

SUMMER
Litha

SUMMER TURNS TO AUTUMN
Lammas

• **MAYING CELEBRATIONS**
Moveable: *Historical and modern celebrations of May, including processions, maypoles and the crowning of May Queens*

• **BELTANE**
May 1: *Celtic fire festival marking the mid-point between Spring and Summer*

• **WALPURGIS NIGHT**
April 30: *Late-night bonfire rituals celebrate the beginning of summer in northern Europe*

• **KAWONI**
April: *Cherokee month of flowers, beginning on the new moon*

• **HANAMI**
April–May: *Cherry blossom parties take place in Japanese public parks and gardens*

• **FLORIFERTUM**
May 1–5: *Ancient Roman flower festivities in honour of the Spring goddesses Flora and Maia*

55

A Blanket of Flowers

May in the northern hemisphere is a magnificent prelude to Summer — loud with birdsong (including the trills of the nightingale), and rich in flowers and blossom.

• • • • •

In ancient Rome, May 1–5 was Florifertum (the Festival of Flowers), beginning with Floralia on May 1. These festivities were dedicated to Flora, goddess of flowers and the Spring. Offerings of milk and honey were laid out to seek her protection for the blossoming plants. Participants dressed in multi-coloured clothes and garlands to imitate the bright colours of nature, and let loose captured hares and goats to symbolize fertility.

The goddess Flora, clothed in flowers, painted by Sandro Botticelli, c.1482.

CHERRY BLOSSOM

Flower festivals have also been celebrated in Japan for hundreds of years. In the 7th century, Heian-period courtiers wrote poems in which they meditated on the beauty and transience of the delicate cherry blossom (*sakura*). Lively cherry blossom parties (Hanami), with wine and poetry readings, still take place in modern Japan — in May in the north, in January or February in the south, but mostly in March or April. Cherry blossom is sometimes considered to be the national flower of Japan, and also symbolizes the brief, intense life of the samurai warrior.

FLOWER MOON

Native American tradition associates flowers with late Spring. The Cherokee speak of the Month of the Flower Moon. But less decorative sides of nature also played their part with these peoples. The Knee Deep dance (*dustu*) was perfomed in late Spring, inspired by a small frog which appeared at this time of year.

"The flowers appear on the earth . . . and the voice of the turtledove is heard in our land."

SONG OF SOLOMON 2.12

Banishing the Darkness

Beltane is a transitional time, when the boundaries falter between light and dark, life and death, and the natural and supernatural worlds — and spirits walk the Earth.

· · · · ·

In Celtic lore the spirits from the "dark half" of the year enjoyed a last night of freedom at Beltane, causing havoc across the human world. In Gaelic legend, mischievous fairies, known as the *doine sidhe* ("the people of the *sidhe* mounds") could travel the Earth at Beltane. To protect themselves and their livestock from these fairies and evil spirits, people in Ireland and Scotland decorated their houses with fresh greenery at the beginning of May, and nailed crosses of newly cut wood to their houses and barns.

The ancient Romans, too, chose the beginning of May to placate wandering spirits (*lemures*), making offerings, conducting rituals and praying to the godess Maia at their festival of Lemuria. At this event, Vestal Virgins prepared a sacred mixture of grain and salt known as *mola salsa*, which was offered to the spirits. In Book V of *Fasti* (The

Eternal Battle

Gwayn ap Nudd, the Celtic god of the Underworld, and his rival Gwythr ap Greidawl, fought over the maiden Creiddylad every May Day. In some versions of this myth their battle was settled by King Arthur, who decreed that they must fight until Doomsday. Whoever won Creiddylad's hand on that day would get to keep her forever. Their struggle symbolized the cyclical contest between the light and dark halves of the Celtic year.

Yearly Calendar), the poet Ovid recorded how the head of the household would rise at midnight to summon restless family ghosts, whose spirits could be trapped inside black beans and banished with the incantation *Manes exite paterni*, which translates as "Go forth, ancestral spirits".

WALPURGIS NIGHT

In northern Europe, an important late Spring festival is Walpurgis Night, marked with bonfires and late-night events in Germany, Sweden, Finland and Estonia, among other countries. Although not a Christian festival in modern times, Walpurgis Night is named for a Saxon saint and missionary, Walpurga.

In Germany, *Walpurgisnacht* falls on the evening of April 30. Revellers, often dressed as witches with broomsticks and pointed hats, light bonfires and await the dawn, when the forces of dark symbolically bow to the forces of light. The Brocken, the highest peak in the Harz Mountains, is the focal point of German celebrations – Goethe's *Faust* mentions witches riding there on Walpurgis Night, accompanied by Mephistopheles and Faust himself.

A Walpurgisnacht *bonfire lights up the darkness in Germany. Bonfires lit at this time of year symbolize purifying light and the banishment of dark forces.*

Hawthorn: the Fairy Tree

The flowers of the hawthorn plant herald the Summer, and boughs of this May blossom were used in many early Summer rituals of celebration and protection.

• • • • •

An old British saying states, "Cast not a clout till may be out" – a warning not to throw away warm clothing until may blossom appears, as only then is good weather assured. The word "hawthorn" comes from the Anglo-Saxon *haegthorn* (hedge thorn). It was used to make charms to ward off danger at this transitional time: its prickly spines and its use as a hedging plant gave it associations with protection. As far apart as Ireland and Greece, its blossom was used in bridal bouquets, to symbolically protect a couple on their journey through life.

FAIRY LEGENDS

Hawthorn trees are associated with many of Beltane's fairy legends, as they were thought to be portals to the fairy realm, especially when they grew in the sacred triad of "oak, ash and thorn". Hanging ribbons or shreds of clothing onto hawthorns placated any passing fairies. In medieval Europe, people hung hawthorn branches on a child's cradle to prevent the baby from being stolen by fairies and replaced with a changeling. The Scottish poet True Thomas (Thomas of Ercildoune) is said to have met the queen of fairyland under a hawthorn tree on May 1: she took him to fairyland for seven years, and he returned with the gift of prophecy.

Two youths cut down leafy branches in this 18th-century manuscript. The branches would have been used for decoration and seasonal festivities.

MEDIEVAL LORE

May Day festivities appear frequently in medieval literature. In Arthurian legend, Queen Guinevere was kidnapped by the mysterious "Lord of the Summer Country" while taking part in May Day celebrations. She was rescued by Lancelot, and they declared their love for one another. The name of a fearsome Welsh giant, Ysbaddadon Pen Cawr, means "Hawthorn-head Giant"; he had a beautiful daughter, Olwen, in whose footsteps trefoil flowers blossomed.

The Glastonbury Thorn

The famous "Holy Thorn" tree in the grounds of Glastonbury Abbey, England, is a species of hawthorn which flowers at Christmas and in May. In the Middle Ages, its dual flowering was held to be miraculous. It was related to the (apocryphal) belief that the original thorn grew from the staff of Joseph of Arimathea, the saint who, according to the Gospel of Mark, requested Jesus' body from Pontius Pilate and donated his own grave for Jesus' burial. Joseph was also credited with being instrumental in the establishment of Christianity in Britain. However, there is no evidence that Joseph ever visited Europe, and one possibility is that the hawthorn's Pagan associations with protection were given a Christian slant. The original tree was cut down and burnt in the English Civil War as an idolatrous relic – the tree that stands today is a distant descendant, grown from cuttings. A spray of the Glastonbury thorn is still sent as a gift to the monarch of England each Christmas.

Horned Gods and May Games

Figures associated with the transition from Spring to Summer include the horned god Cernunnos and Robin Hood. Along with the maypoles that appear at this time of year, they are associated with fertility and communal celebration.

· · · · ·

In Spring and Summer in the fertile valley of Val Camonica, Italy, prehistoric people hunted game and collected wild foods such as honey. They recorded these activities there, in rock art carvings which are now thousands of years old. Presiding over everything is an immense horned figure: Cernunnos, a deity particularly associated with Beltane and the beginning of Summer, who was worshipped throughout Britain, Gaul and northern Italy.

Some images of Cernunnos, such as a bronze figure from Etang-sur-Arroux, France, have holes in their heads. Antlers were inserted into these holes in Spring and removed during the Winter, in rites reflecting Cernunnos's status as the lord of nature, at the height of his powers in early Summer. A famous representation of Cernunnos dating back to the 3rd century BCE appears on the Gundestrup Cauldron, found in Denmark in 1891 (illustrated opposite). He has two torcs, indicating his power and divinity, and he holds a ram-headed snake, a Celtic symbol of the regeneration of nature.

MAY GAMES AND ROBIN HOOD

Boisterous communal rituals reflected the metaphorical battle between order and chaos at the onset of Summer. Robin Hood Games, when entire villages joined in feasting, processions and competitions, took place in May in Britain during the 15th and 16th centuries. They marked the regeneration of the surrounding forest land – a source of firewood, building materials and fodder for animals. Villagers acted out the adventures of Robin Hood, the benevolent outlaw, and his men, and sometimes these games became wild, attracting the disapproval of local priests and landlords.

THE MAYPOLE

Flower- and ribbon-bedecked maypoles, symbols of fertility and the focus for community celebrations, are still widely seen on village greens and at country fairs. Well established in Europe by the 14th century, maypoles also reflect the symbolism of the World Tree, common to many cultures including Nordic and Indian, which bridged the gap between heaven and Earth. Dancing around the maypole symbolized rejoicing at the return of the vegetation spirit, and also youth and fertility. Young men and women intertwined ribbons as they danced around the pole, and a poet writing in 1618 recorded them exchanging "a smiling kiss at every turning".

Erecting a maypole is still a shared project today in Bavaria, and emblems of clubs and societies who contribute are attached to the pole as well as the customary flowers. In the Czech Republic, villages compete to erect the tallest *maj* (maypole).

Cernunnos is depicted on the Gundestrup Cauldron sitting in a typical cross-legged position. His antlers, and those of the deer beside him, indicate his status as a Summer deity: deer shed their antlers seasonally.

The Green Man

For centuries, a mysterious figure known as the Green Man has appeared in May Day folk plays, festivals and fairs all over Europe, as well as on the walls, pillars and ceilings of churches – with convincing analogies outside Europe, too.

• • • • •

May Day celebrations today are often led by a "May Queen", a young girl who represents purity and the potential for growth. Her consort is the "Green Man". He symbolizes the spirit of vegetation and is crowned by the May Queen in a ceremony known as "Fetching in the May", which marks the beginning of Summer. Jack-in-the-Green, a man "trapped" inside a wooden cage decorated with leaves and flowers, also appeared at May Day revels in the 18th century. Jack disrupted social order in order to settle local

The Green Man in Islam

The Romance of Alexander is a collection of the legendary adventures of Alexander the Great. Among the many characters he meets is Al-Khidr, a popular saintly figure in Islamic tradition. Alexander crossed the Land of Darkness with Al-Khidr searching for the water of life, at the edge of the world. The wise Al-Khidr reached this goal, although the worldly king failed to do so. After Al-Khidr bathed here, he became entirely green as a symbol of his immortality; wherever he walked the earth turned green under his feet.

quarrels, often wearing comical disguise or deploying practical jokes.

GREEN MEN AND THE CHURCH

Architectural depictions of a human face made of leaves, emerging from foliage or with greenery growing from its mouth, have survived in religious locations including St Paul's in London and Chartres in France (and even Jain temples in Rajasthan, India). These are also known as "Green Men", but their origin remains a mystery. It is unlikely

The Green Man appears as a ceiling boss in Norwich Cathedral (c.1300), in eastern England. It has been suggested by some that this emblem was used as a symbol of regeneration following the Black Death.

that they are Pagan images – indeed the motif seems to have been created for Christian churches. Church imagery was a key means of communication in an age when few were literate, and it is possible that the Green Man made it clear that uneducated woodlanders were welcome in the house of God.

Summer
June 21 – July 31

"Give me the splendid silent sun with all his beams full-dazzling."

WALT WHITMAN (1819–1892)

• • • • •

Summer Solstice 68
Sun, Light and Fire 70
Summer in the Zodiac 74
A Time to Pause 76
The Oak: King of the Woods 78
Solstice Sites 80

Summer Solstice

Midsummer's Day, the longest of the year, falls on June 21 or 22 in the northern hemisphere (December 21 or 22 in the southern). This is the Summer Solstice, marking the beginning of Summer in the Wheel of the Year.

• • • • •

The word "solstice" is derived from the Latin words *sol*, meaning sun, and *sistere* meaning "cause to stand still". As the days advance toward the solstice, the sun gets progressively higher in the sky, until the day it reaches its maximum height: the following day it will climax a little lower, as the days start to shorten again. The farther from the Equator you are, the more daylight you experience: indeed, beyond the latitude of 66°30', there is 24-hour sunlight. The Summer Solstice tends to be celebrated most energetically in locations where this life-giving daylight lasts longest, and where the contrast between Winter and Summer is therefore most marked.

Honouring Mary and Ezili

Among the celebrations that take place during Midsummer is the feast of Our Lady of Mount Carmel. Falling on July 16, the day that the Virgin Mary appeared in a vision to the founder of the Carmelite order, St Simon Stock, it is marked with masses and processions across the Christian world. In Haiti, the same day is dedicated to Mary's *lwa* (voodoo spirit) counterpart, Ezili, who, like Mary, is a goddess of motherhood and protection. Hundreds of pilgrims travel to the Saut d'Eau waterfalls in Haiti on this day to take "luck baths", and ask Ezili and other *lwas* for good fortune and an abundant harvest.

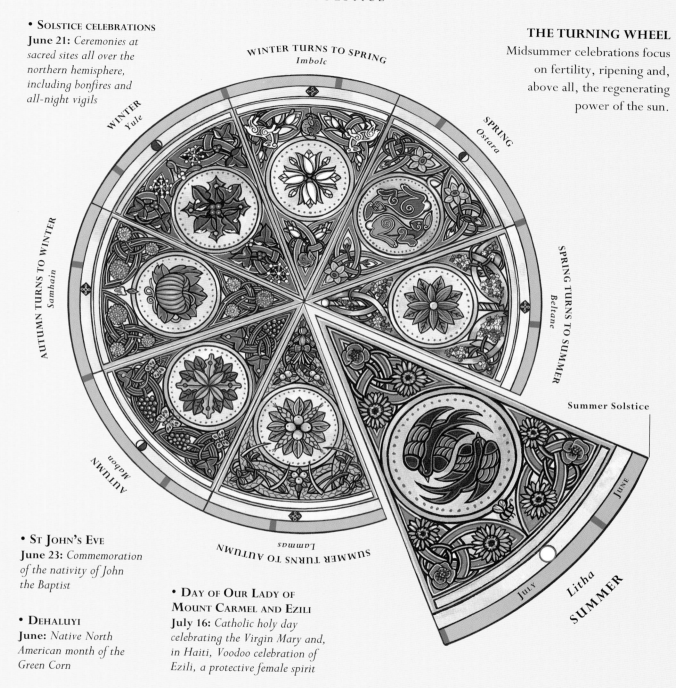

- **SOLSTICE CELEBRATIONS**
June 21: *Ceremonies at sacred sites all over the northern hemisphere, including bonfires and all-night vigils*

THE TURNING WHEEL
Midsummer celebrations focus on fertility, ripening and, above all, the regenerating power of the sun.

WINTER TURNS TO SPRING
Imbolc

WINTER
Yule

SPRING
Ostara

AUTUMN TURNS TO WINTER
Samhain

SPRING TURNS TO SUMMER
Beltane

AUTUMN
Mabon

Summer Solstice

SUMMER TURNS TO AUTUMN
Lammas

JUNE

JULY

Litha
SUMMER

- **ST JOHN'S EVE**
June 23: *Commemoration of the nativity of John the Baptist*

- **DEHALUYI**
June: *Native North American month of the Green Corn*

- **DAY OF OUR LADY OF MOUNT CARMEL AND EZILI**
July 16: *Catholic holy day celebrating the Virgin Mary and, in Haiti, Voodoo celebration of Ezili, a protective female spirit*

Sun, Light and Fire

Midsummer sunlight, even in temperate climes, can be powerful and energizing.
Flames and fire, associated with the sun, have been a major feature of Midsummer
celebrations since time immemorial.

• • • • •

The link between the sun and flames is apparent in the number of bonfire traditions associated with Midsummer. As well as a celebration, these fires are an offering: the sun's energy will wane as the Winter Solstice approaches, so lighting fires is a way of bolstering the sun's power, of giving something back by feeding its flames from our own energy. Midsummer fires are lit to symbolize and promote fertility, strength and good fortune for the coming harvest. In several countries, including Germany, young men leap over the bonfires, and the height of their jumps is said to presage the height of

Rolling Sunwheels

The sun is often represented as a wheel, and Midsummer sun rituals include rolling burning wheels downhill to represent the declining power of the sun from this time on. Tradition has it that if the wheel continues to burn all the way down, the harvest will be good. However, if the fire goes out, the crops may fail. Sunwheels are still rolled down hills in some British towns and villages, and the custom is particularly strong in Yorkshire. In Latvia, a *pundele* (a barrel or wheel soaked in tar and wrapped in straw) is placed on top of a pole at the crest of a hill and set alight for the same symbolic reasons.

"The sun does not shine for a few trees
and flowers, but for the wide world's joy."

HENRY WARD BEECHER (1813–1887)

the coming crops. Later, when the fires die down, people run over the embers to make sure that they are blessed with good luck in the coming months.

UP ALL NIGHT

All-night vigils are also widespread on Midsummer's Eve. People in countries as diverse as Japan, Britain and Norway stay awake until midnight or even right through this, the shortest night of the year, to welcome in the longest day at dawn. An old British folktale claims that the spirits of those doomed to die during the coming year wander abroad on this night. Many people would stay awake until dawn, in order to guarantee that their spirit was given no chance to slip away.

ST JOHN'S EVE

For many countries in Europe, such as Italy, Lithuania, Latvia, Norway, Finland and Sweden, June 23, just a day or two after Midsummer's Eve, is St John's Eve – a festival that has largely disappeared from the ceremonial calendar in Britain and America. This day commemorates the Nativity of John the Baptist (approximately six months before the birth of Christ, which coincides with the Winter Solstice).

In Latvia, the festival of Jani (from Janis, the Latvian for John) is still hugely popular; in fact, it is a national holiday. Fires are lit in advance of sunset on the day before the solstice, and are kept burning by people who stay awake through the night. Women weave wreaths of flowering herbs and other

Two girls weave Summer flowers into wreaths for their hair in this 15th-century French manuscript. Wreaths are still commonly worn at Midsummer in Europe.

Marking the Midnight Sun

In far northern latitudes, the sun does not set from mid-May until late July. In parts of Sweden, Finland, Norway and throughout Iceland, there is 24-hour sunlight at Midsummer. People go there to enjoy the strange sensation of nighttime daylight – the "Midnight Sun". The eerie atmosphere of these "white nights" has also led to Midsummer's Eve being associated with magic and fortune-telling. Girls used to eat salted porridge so that their future husband would bring them water to drink in their dreams, and keep watch at springs for a reflection of their future lover in the water. On Midsummer's Eve in Sweden, people visit the countryside to dress poles with leaves and flowers, and to dance and feast with families and friends. The "White Nights" of St Petersburg in Russia are a metropolitan version of the same experience, with midnight promenades along the city's elegant avenues.

plants, and wear them as crowns. Large choirs sing traditional Midsummer folk songs called *ligotne*, named for the characteristic refrain of *ligo, ligo*, meaning "good cheer".

Midsummer marks the end of the ploughing, sowing and weeding work in the fields, and the beginning of the harvesting season. To mark this, celebrants drink freshly brewed beer and eat *Janu* cheese, asking for blessings on the harvest.

In Finland, the festivities held in honour of St John are known as Juhannus. On the "museum island" of Seurasaari, close to the capital of Helsinki, elaborate Midsummer celebrations have taken place for more than 50 years. Visitors watch (and participate in) Finnish folk dances, musicians play traditional songs, dramatic bonfires are lit, and rowing races are contested on the water surrounding the island. In Denmark, Sankt Hans Aften (St John's Eve) was an official holiday until 1770, and today it is marked with fires and picnics held on beaches and the banks of lakes and rivers, where revellers sing the traditional *Midsommervise* (Midsummer Verse), *Vi Elsker Vort Land* ("We Love Our Land").

Summer in the Zodiac

The sun moves from Cancer (a water sign) into Leo (a fire sign) around July 23. So, as well as its associations with fire, owing to the strength of the sun at this time of year, the Summer carries important water symbolism.

• • • • •

The Nile floods, essential for farming, were a phenomenon of Midsummer – linking this season with water imagery in Egypt's mythology. The appearance of the constellation of Leo in the night sky was an indication that the inundation was imminent. (Today, Leo appears in the night sky in Spring in the northern hemisphere, because the Earth has wobbled on its axis over the millennia.) Thus, Leo, and lions, became symbolically aligned with water, even though Leo is a fire sign. This is why lion heads were carved on canal gates in ancient Egypt – a decoration Greek and Roman architects adopted for their fountains.

This 14th-century engraving shows a king-like personification of the sun, attended by a lion representing Leo, one of the astrological fire signs.

So the constellation of Leo was wedded to the idea of water. However, it was also strongly linked with the sun in the Mesopotamian and Egyptian world-view. The most luminous star in the constellation was (and is) Regulus, meaning "little king". Located at the lion's heart, Regulus was used by the Mesopotamians to mark the Summer Solstice: the sun's passage at midday through its area of the sky coincided with the Summer Solstice. Regulus was one of four "marker" stars equally spaced around the "ecliptic", the imaginary plane on which all the planets orbit the sun – the other three marked the Winter Solstice and the two equinoxes.

Lion Symbols

The Egyptian god Aker, the god of the horizon who opened the gates of the Underworld, appears in ancient manuscripts as two magnificent lions, one looking east and the other west, with the sun between them. From Aker to Aslan (the lion who represents Christ in C.S. Lewis's *Chronicles of Narnia*), the lion has been associated with strength, energy and kingship – like the sun, whose golden rays are suggested by the lion's mane. In the Book of Exodus, Jacob's son Judah is described as being "like a lion", and his tribe's symbol was a lion. The Sphinx, with a lion's body and a human head, derives its name from the Egyptian *Sheshep-ankh*, which translates as "the living image of the sun-like god".

A Time to Pause

With the sun high in the sky and a good chance of glorious weather, Midsummer has always been regarded as a time of rest and relaxation for agricultural communities, between the hard work of sowing and planting, and the labour of the harvest.

• • • • •

As summer begins, the weather is often mild and settled. Midsummer is traditionally a time for holidays, outdoor gatherings and festivals – not to mention weddings (see box, opposite). Before the advent of the regular summer vacation, people spent the leisure hours of summer around home, and this encouraged communal enjoyments, making the most of long evenings. Fishing, hunting, riding, athletic sports, bathing and ball games loomed large, and village fairs were a focus of social cohesion.

MONTH OF THE GREEN CORN

In America, the staple crop of maize begins to ripen around Midsummer. In Native American tradition, the first appearance of the maize tassels marks the Month of the Green Corn, officially called Dehaluyi, and celebrated throughout June. At this

A detail from a 15th-century French manuscript shows children enjoying their leisure, bathing in a ford at Midsummer. The sign of Cancer appears above them, framed by the sun, to mark the season.

76

time, many tribes make plans for the future and look ahead to the coming harvest. Some use this quieter period before harvest begins to give something to the community, by performing acts of charity.

HEALING LIGHT

The strength of the sun at this time of year is sometimes believed to imbue plants with healing qualities. On Midsummer's Day in ancient Denmark, women would gather the herbs for their healing potions for the rest of the year. People also bathed in and drank the healing waters of lakes that captured the Midsummer sunshine, to gain health and good fortune.

One plant saturated with the sun's healing energy is St John's Wort, so named because according to legend it flowered on St John's Day (June 24). Also known as "chase devil", St John's Wort flowers harvested at Midsummer can be dried and kept until winter when, made into a tea, they are believed to chase away Winter blues.

June Weddings

There are many love rituals associated with Midsummer. One British folk tradition states that if a young girl picks a sprig of St John's Wort on Midsummer's Eve and it is still fresh in the morning, she will soon marry. The month of June is, in fact, named after Juno, the Roman goddess of marriage and motherhood, and June has historically been a time associated with weddings. This is partially due to the strength of the sun at this time of year: romantic love can be compared to the strong, beating heart of Summer rather than the gentler, blossoming love of Spring. In addition, as farming communities paused at Midsummer, between planting and the harvest, it was a less demanding time in which workers could leave the fields with sufficient leisure to hold a wedding celebration and enjoy the honeymoon that followed. The word "honeymoon" relates to the abundance of honey available at this time of year – a delicacy eaten at medieval European wedding feasts.

The Oak: King of the Woods

Summer is the season when the woodlands, with their broad-leaved trees, are shady and mysterious. In Celtic tradition, the most important tree in the Summer woods is the oak, which the druids called the King of the Woods.

• • • • •

According to many classical writers, druids, the priests of Celtic societies, held rituals beneath the spreading branches of the great oaks that marked their sacred groves. The Roman historian Pliny the Elder suggested that the name "druid" was in fact related to the Greek word for oak, *drus*. He also recorded that mistletoe growing on oak trees was sacred to the druids of Gaul: the plant was cut with a golden sickle, and caught before it touched the ground, in a ritual that coincided with the new moon.

The oak's majesty, its longevity (some oaks live for 2,000 years) and its status as the tree most often struck by lightning (owing to a number of characteristics, including its tendency to grow above underground streams) have all given it connections with powerful father-gods. These include Thor and Zeus, who both had power over thunder and lightning, and Mars Silvanus, the woodland aspect of the Roman god Mars.

Modern Pagan rituals at Midsummer re-enact a symbolic battle between the wise Oak King, who rules from Midwinter to Midsummer, and the youthful Holly King. Before the Summer Solstice, the Oak King is always growing in power. Crowned with lush green leaves, he is usually represented as a young man, full of optimism and vitality. At the Summer Solstice, however, the Oak King is defeated by the Holly King, who reigns until the Winter Solstice, when he is, in turn, vanquished by the Oak King. Their cyclical battle reflects the balance between the seasons.

Solstice Sites

Prehistoric monuments with precise solar alignments, including the great standing stones at Stonehenge, provide evidence that observance of the solstices dates back at least several millennia.

• • • • •

While sites such as Fajada Butte in Chaco Canyon, New Mexico, make use of directed sunbeams to "spotlight" carvings on rock walls at sunrise or sunset on the solstices and equinoxes, other sites, such as Callanish in Scotland, are made up of standing stones over which the sun rises or sets at these times of year.

Of all these sacred sites, perhaps the most famous is Stonehenge in Wiltshire,

England. The original site (Stonehenge I) is thought to have been built around 3100BCE, although the present structure (Stonehenge III) probably dates back to *c*.1550BCE. Stonehenge is recognized by NASA as one of the five oldest observatories in the world. One American astronomer even spoke of it as a primitive "computer", used to predict lunar and solar eclipses. 18th-century antiquarians believed that Stonehenge was the central location for Druidic rituals.

Modern Druids still hold Midsummer rites at Stonehenge, and festivities connected with the Summer Solstice have taken place there since at least the 13th century. In 1223 the Bishop of Salisbury denounced the Midsummer events as "vile and indecorous games". Today, up to 30,000 people travel from all over the world to celebrate dawn on Midsummer's Day at Stonehenge. As the sun rises, it aligns dramatically with the huge "Heel Stone", to great rejoicing from the assembled visitors.

Morning sunlight glows on the ancient standing stones of Stonehenge. The stone used to carve them was transported from Welsh mountains more than 240 miles (385km) away, an astonishing feat in c.2100BCE.

Summer
TURNS TO
Autumn
August 1 – September 20

"Harvest will come, and then every farmer's rich."

THOMAS FULLER (1654–1734)

• • • • •

Harvest 84
Remembering Ancestors 86
Crop Deities: Myth and Ritual 88
Lughnasadh 92
Sheaf Ceremonies 94
Death and Rebirth 96

Harvest

The harvest is the time when the Earth's life-giving potential is fulfilled. Relief and gratitude inspire festivities that focus on symbolic produce.

• • • • •

Tradition in northern Europe placed the first day of the harvest on August 1 – mid-way between the Summer Solstice and the Autumn Equinox. Lammas, the Celtic feast day which is the origin of our modern harvest festivals, fell on this day. Lammas was marked with feasting, games and thanksgiving. The word Lammas is derived from the Anglo-Saxon *hlaf-maesse*, meaning loaf mass or "celebration of bread", reflecting the vital importance of the cereal harvest to ancient communities. Soldiers would return from service to help in the fields and the entire community would pull together to make sure that the work was completed. Many country fairs and summer fêtes take place in Europe and America at this time of year, with parallels in other cultures, too.

Harvest Festivals

Modern church festivals feature harvest baskets filled with fruit, bread and seasonal vegetables. These gifts are distributed to the elderly, poor and infirm of the community – a reminder that we should not take the abundance of our harvest for granted, but should be grateful for the good fortune to have enough to give away. Leaving offerings at an altar also serves as a gesture of thanks to God, echoing the ancient tradition of sacrificial ceremonies to the deities who guarded essential crops (see pages 88–91).

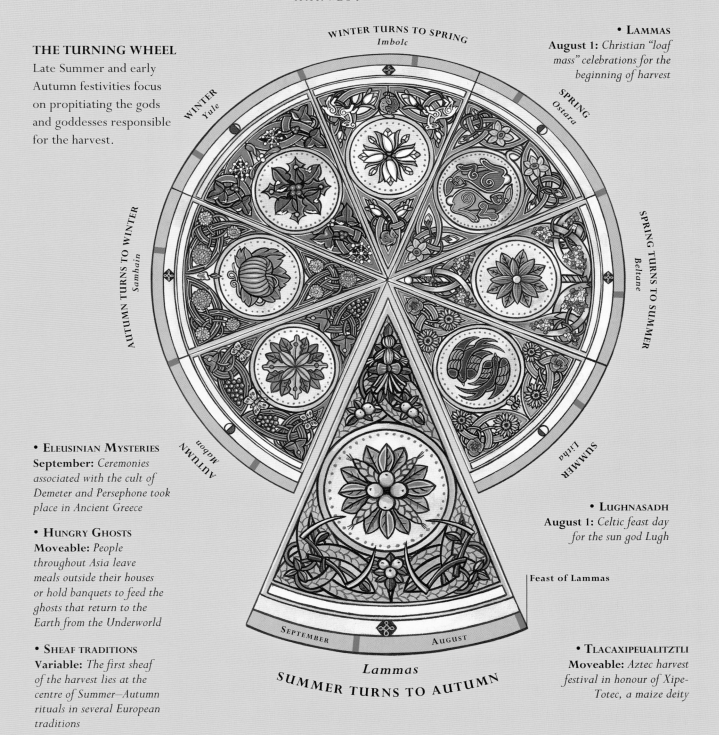

THE TURNING WHEEL
Late Summer and early Autumn festivities focus on propitiating the gods and goddesses responsible for the harvest.

WINTER TURNS TO SPRING
Imbolc

WINTER
Yule

• **LAMMAS**
August 1: *Christian "loaf mass" celebrations for the beginning of harvest*

SPRING
Ostara

AUTUMN TURNS TO WINTER
Samhain

SPRING TURNS TO SUMMER
Beltane

SUMMER
Litha

AUTUMN
Mabon

• **ELEUSINIAN MYSTERIES**
September: *Ceremonies associated with the cult of Demeter and Persephone took place in Ancient Greece*

• **HUNGRY GHOSTS**
Moveable: *People throughout Asia leave meals outside their houses or hold banquets to feed the ghosts that return to the Earth from the Underworld*

• **SHEAF TRADITIONS**
Variable: *The first sheaf of the harvest lies at the centre of Summer–Autumn rituals in several European traditions*

• **LUGHNASADH**
August 1: *Celtic feast day for the sun god Lugh*

Feast of Lammas

SEPTEMBER

AUGUST

Lammas
SUMMER TURNS TO AUTUMN

• **TLACAXIPEUALITZTLI**
Moveable: *Aztec harvest festival in honour of Xipe-Totec, a maize deity*

Remembering Ancestors

As well as the revelry of harvest festivals, there are rituals to contact ghosts and commemorate ancestors — the time of plenty is also a time of spirits.

• • • • •

Some festivals at this time of year mourn dead kinsfolk as well as giving thanks for a successful harvest. Offering up a portion of this harvest to the gods or to our ancestors, and feasting in their honour, helps to remind us of the cycles of nature. The logic is inescapable: beyond the seasonal cycle is a cycle of lifetimes in which all of us participate. And our ancestors, in their wisdom, could be said to be as nourishing to our souls as the harvest is to our bodies.

The Celtic god Lugh is believed to have ordered a commemorative feast for his beloved mother Tailtiu at the beginning of the harvest season, and this is the origin of the Celtic feast-day Lughnasadh

The Hungry Ghosts

At this time of plenty, restless spirits are believed to walk the Earth, in Asian countries, at the Hungry Ghosts Festival. They return to the land of the living from a form of purgatory where they are never fed. In Singapore, people prepare banquets for the hungry ghosts, while in Malaysia, bowls of noodles, sweetmeats, cakes and other treats are left out for them. The festival is known as Yue Lan in China. It begins on the 14th day of the Seventh Moon, and ends at midnight of the 30th day, when the ghosts return to their own domain.

This 12th-century stone relief shows an image of the god Saturn, carrying his emblem of a scythe and accompanied by a sheep.

(see pages 92–93). Games and contests were held at this time elsewhere. The ancient Olympic Games, which the Greeks held between August 6 and September 19 every four years, may originally have been organized to commemorate the deeds of heroes who had died in battle.

The Ga people of Ghana celebrate the Homowo, or "Hooting at Hunger" Festival, on a weekend in August or early September. On the Friday, they commemorate those who have died during the previous year; on the Saturday, celebrations for the abundance of food begin, lasting until Sunday night. Families travel from far afield to gather together, bringing the fruits of their harvest. They eat large quantities of traditional foods including *kpekpele* (steamed fermented corn meal). On the Saturday of the celebratory weekend, tribal chiefs and the heads of families ritually sprinkle a little *kpekpele* in special places, to please the ancestors and appease the gods.

SATURN AND HIS SCYTHE

Roman reliefs often feature an old man with a scythe – this is Saturn, who was a god of agriculture, the harvest and of barley in particular. In Roman mythology, his wife was the goddess Ops, whose name means "plenty"; she was associated with Ceres (see page 88). Saturn was also identified with the Greek god Kronos (whose name is etymologically related to "chronology"). He eventually evolved into the modern figure of Old Father Time. His scythe – and his age – both give him associations with the transition from Summer to Autumn.

Crop Deities: Myth and Ritual

As Summer turns to Autumn, various cultures revere those deities who preside over the harvest — many of whom are personified by sheaves of corn. These gods and (more often) goddesses include Demeter, Hun Hunahpu and Xipe-Totec.

· · · · ·

In early Autumn every year in ancient Greece, a procession took place from Athens to Eleusis, 12 miles (20km) to the east. This was part of the Greater Mysteries, a nine-day festival that was key to the Eleusinian mystery religion, sacred to the nature goddess Demeter (known in Roman myth as Ceres, whose name is the root of the word "cereal"). This goddess was particularly connected with the vegetation cycle and the harvest. Her name may derive from *De meter*, meaning "barley mother", or *Ge meter*, meaning "Earth mother".

The Eleusinian mystery religion was open to everyone, so long as they spoke Greek and had never killed another human being. The exact details of the various ceremonies are unknown, as participants had to maintain secrecy on pain of death; but the Greek historian Hippolytus claimed that during the Greater Mysteries, an ear of corn reaped in silence was displayed to initiates. This was used to symbolize life and the latent life-energy in all plants.

CORN GODDESSES

Demeter was the mother aspect of a triple goddess (see page 29) whose other aspects were Persephone (maiden) and the Moon goddess Hecate (crone). Persephone's descent into the Underworld (for the full version of the Persephone myth, see page 143) symbolizes the death of the Summer crops and their retreat into the earth. Hecate also had a festival dedicated to her, celebrated on August 29 in Greece

Harvested maize cobs dry in the sun on a farm in Mexico. Maize (known as corn in America) was a staple crop for both North and South American peoples.

and August 13 in Rome. Traditionally a moon goddess, Hecate was invoked for the protection of the ripening grain and fruit, which are particularly vulnerable to damage from high winds and storms in the last weeks before harvest. Reflecting the transitional feeling of this time of year, Hecate was also a mediator between life and death, and statues depicting her often stood at crossroads in ancient Greece and Rome.

In the Zodiac, early Autumn is ruled by Virgo (August 24 – September 23), the only female human figure in sun-sign astrology. She is often depicted holding a sheaf of corn,

Peasants harvest wheat in this 14th-century Italian manuscript. The figure on the left impersonates a grain deity, to bring good luck to the harvest.

and the symbolism associated with the sign can be traced back to ancient Mesopotamia.

CELEBRATING MAIZE

The Mayan creator god Hun Hunahpu ruled over maize, the most important Mayan crop. He was released from the Underworld by his sons, the "Hero Twins", and presided over the Cosmic Tree, the axis of the world whose green colour symbolized fertility.

The Aztecs also celebrated harvest, at their festival of Tlacaxipeualiztli, in honour of their vegetation god, Xipe-Totec ("the flayed one"), often depicted dressed in the skin of a sacrificial victim. Warriors would wear the skin for several days, and eventually it hardened, shrank and split to reveal their healthy bodies. This represented the idea that as one year's crops were cut down, there was a new harvest lying in wait in the seeds under the soil; it also reflected the way in which maize seeds lose old skin when new growth bursts through.

The harvest season is an important time in modern Native American tradition, celebrated by tribes including the Cherokee, Creek, Seminole and Iroquois. In August, the Cherokee Green Corn Ceremony takes place (it was formerly held in July). None of the new corn can be consumed before rituals of purification and forgiveness are performed, as well as a green corn dance to give thanks to the Great Spirit or Great Mother. Minor transgressions are forgiven at council meetings. September is the Cherokee Nut Moon, but early in this month, the Ripe Corn Moon Festival is held to propitiate Selu, the spirit of the corn, who is also identified with the First Woman in Cherokee tradition.

The Three Sisters

In Native American tradition, three essential, life-sustaining crops – corn, beans and squash – were known as the Three Sisters. These were grown together – and still are today, in a practice known as companion planting. The bean vines provide nitrogen to nourish the corn, and use the tall corn stalks as poles to grow around. The squashes grow at the base of the other plants, and provide shade to keep the ground moist and weeds to a minimum.

Lughnasadh

Another, older name for the Lammas festival on August 1 is Lughnasadh — the commemoration of the Celtic god Lugh, also known as Lug or Llew. His mythology is deeply entwined with agricultural traditions.

· · · · ·

Lúnasa is still the name given to August in Irish Gaelic; in Scots Gaelic, it is known as Lunasda. According to Celtic legend, Lugh's foster mother, the tribal queen Tailtiu, and her people were defeated by the Tuatha De Dannan, a clan of gods who invaded ancient Ireland. Tailtiu was forced to clear a vast forest in order to plant grain, and, in the end, she died of exhaustion.

Lugh decreed that a feast in Tailtiu's honour, called Lughnasadh, should be held each year at the start of the harvest season.

Striking Bargains at the Fair

One possible root of the word "Lugh" is the Celtic word *lugio*, meaning oath. At Lammas fairs across Europe during the 15th and 16th centuries, young couples would agree to undertake a trial marriage, lasting for a year and a day. If, by the end of this period, the couple felt that the partnership was not to their liking, they were free to go their separate ways. In many areas of Europe, country fairs were held just after the harvest specifically for the purposes of either this type of matchmaking or hiring workers. Labourers were taken on for the upcoming season, and financial arrangements were made. Aspects of these fairs survive in autumn country events today all across Europe and North America.

Legend has it that the first feast of Lughnasadh was held where Tailtiu was buried, and that it included games and contests of skill as well as a banquet. Dancing, feasting, the sacrifice of a sacred animal and competitive games are therefore *all* at the centre of Lughnasadh in Celtic tradition. Today's competitions at country fairs – to weave baskets, bake the best cake or grow the largest vegetable – are a lingering vestige of these contests.

Loch Maree and the snow-capped peak of Slioch in the Scottish Highlands. Isle Maree, at the left of the photograph, was a site of Lughnasadh celebrations.

LUGH AND THE HARVEST CYCLE

Lugh defeated the monstrous Balor of the Evil Eye, whose gaze burned up everything it fell upon, at the great battle of Mag Tuired. After his victory, Lugh forced Bres, the usurper king of Ireland who was originally a god of agriculture, to regulate the timing of harvest. Each August 1, Lugh entered into a ritual marriage with the goddess of the land and transferred to her his solar strength, which diminished with the season, to ensure the ripening of the crops. Medieval scribes associated Lugh's name with light.

Sheaf Ceremonies

The last, or first, sheaf of wheat or corn harvested has always had special importance to European farming communities, so various rituals have developed around it.

• • • • •

In many traditions, the last sheaf in each field was left standing as the grains were harvested. Sometimes, this sheaf was burned and its ashes scattered over the fields, while in others it was used to make a corn "dolly" (shown, right), which was buried, burned as an offering or kept until the following Spring to safeguard the land's fertility. The *first* sheaf was at the centre of some Celtic "first fruits" festivities: in the Scottish Hebrides, people rose early on August 15, the festival of the Assumption of the Virgin Mary, to gather the first ripened corn and make it into a celebratory bread known as a "bannock".

CORN DOLLIES

In Celtic and Pictish custom, each year the first farmer to complete his harvest made a corn dolly from part of his crop. He gave it to the next farmer to finish his harvest, and so on. The last farmer to finish then guarded the corn dolly throughout the winter months. The enduring popularity of corn dollies across the world testifies to the importance of grain, and the desire to personify the crop, often in female form.

In Brittany, the harvest doll is known as the Mother Sheaf; in Poland, she is called Baba, or Grandmother; and in Germany, she is the Kornmutter, or Corn Mother. No matter what name she has, the form and traditions remain the same, and corn dollies are still made and sold at fairs today.

In other traditions, the fertility and vigour of the spirit of the corn was symbolized by a goat. In Grenoble, France, for example, a live goat decorated with flowers and ribbons was let loose in the fields just before the harvest began. It was then caught, killed and eaten at the harvest supper.

"*In harvest time, harvest folk, servants and all*
Should make altogether good cheer in the hall."

THOMAS TUSSER (1524–1580)

Death and Rebirth

The observance of nature was extremely important in ancient Egypt and Mesopotamia, where the fields were re-seeded in Autumn, giving rise to several myths, which often centred on the death and resurrection of a god.

● ● ● ● ●

Ancient Egyptian farmers sang a song over the first sheaves of corn to be harvested, which the Greeks called the *Maneros*, or *Ailinus* (from *ai lanu*, or "Woe to us" in Egyptian). The song was simultaneously a lament for the death of the corn spirit and a prayer for its safe return.

The level of the Nile rose in Midsummer, and flood water was channelled through a network of canals and dykes to reach the fields. The Egyptians called this period *akhet* ("the inundation"). As the floods subsided in September, leaving behind fertile silt, farmers would plough the land and sow the next year's seed. It was a precarious livelihood, as drought or over-flooding — both leading to famine — were serious threats. As a safeguard, the early Egyptian farmers worshipped Osiris, god of the corn, the Nile floods, the Underworld and the moon (whose phases controlled the tides, and hence the floods).

Effigies of Osiris made of paste and barley were watered until the grain sprouted, and were then set with candles and floated down the Nile as part of these seasonal ceremonies. Osiris is often represented as a mummy sprouting corn – life coming from death – or with a green tinge to his skin, a reference to his power over the resurrection of life, and vegetation. Corn effigies were often buried in Egyptian tombs.

RESURRECTION

According to the 1st-century historian Plutarch, Osiris was originally a human king who ruled wisely and brought knowledge of agriculture to the Egyptians. His brother Seth became jealous and murdered him by tricking him into lying in a coffin, which was then sealed and thrown into the Nile.

Osiris holds his emblems of a flail and crook, both used in agriculture – the flail was used to thresh crops, the crook to herd sheep. Below his right arm appears a cross-shaped ankh, *the Egyptian hieroglyph for "life".*

Osiris drowned, and the coffin floated away to Byblos, in what is now Lebanon. After a long search, Osiris's sister-wife Isis found her husband's corpse and brought it back to Egypt. Enraged, Seth then dismembered Osiris's body, scattering the parts across Egypt. Isis discovered the pieces of Osiris's body and resurrected her husband. After a series of struggles with Seth, a tribunal of divine judges decreed that Osiris should be restored to life not as a living king, but as king and judge of the dead in the Underworld.

ISHTAR AND TAMMUZ

This theme of rebirth is also illustrated by the tale of Ishtar, the Sumerian goddess of love and war, and her lover Tammuz, the god of vegetation. There are different versions of the myth, but most agree that in the Autumn, Ishtar goes down into the Underworld. While Tammuz mourns for her, animals do not mate and the crops do not grow, until she is returned to the surface. In another version, Tammuz is called Duzumi, and he is the one who dies at harvest time and descends into the Underworld. Inanna (Ishtar) rescues him, but he is only allowed to remain for six months of each year. Duzumi's period on Earth corresponds with the Summer, when Inanna is happy and nature blooms; when he is gone, she mourns and Winter reigns once more.

Autumn

September 21 – October 30

"There is a harmony in Autumn,
and a lustre in its sky . . ."

PERCY BYSSHE SHELLEY (1792–1822)

Autumn Equinox 100
Marking Equinox and Harvest 102
Rosh Hashanah to Sukkot 104
Moon Cakes and Lanterns 106
Celebrating the Vines 108
Dying Light 110

Autumn Equinox

At the Autumn Equinox, day and night are once again exactly equal in length. Their precise balance is reflected in the theme of justice associated with this season.

• • • • •

Mabon, as the Autumn Equinox is known in the Wheel of the Year, falls at the mid-point of the harvest season which began at Lammas (August 1) and will end at Samhain (October 31). For the first time since the Spring Equinox, the powers of darkness start to dominate as nights grow longer and Winter begins to cast its shadow.

Bright constellations including Taurus, Cassiopeia, Pegasus and Ursa Minor reappear in the night sky. Libra, represented by a set of scales and associated with the blind figure of Justice, rules this period in astrology. As the harvest season draws to a close, societies reflect on the work they have accomplished, as they lay down stores for Winter.

Month of the Ivy Moon

The full moon after the Autumn Equinox is the first day of the month of Ivy in the Pagan tree calendar (see pages 146–7). Ivy is a symbol of endurance, as it is an evergreen that grows on dead trees and derelict buildings. In a version of the tale of Tristan and Isolde, King Arthur tells Isolde that she must live with her husband, King Mark, for half the year. Mark chooses the season when the trees are bare, but Isolde points out that ivy never loses its leaves, so she can stay with her lover, Tristan, forever. In Celtic folklore, the plant was a gateway to the fairy world: ivy often attracts butterflies, said to be fairies' earthly form.

THE TURNING WHEEL
Celebrations at Autumn
focus on the harvested crops,
particularly wine, and on
justice and balance.

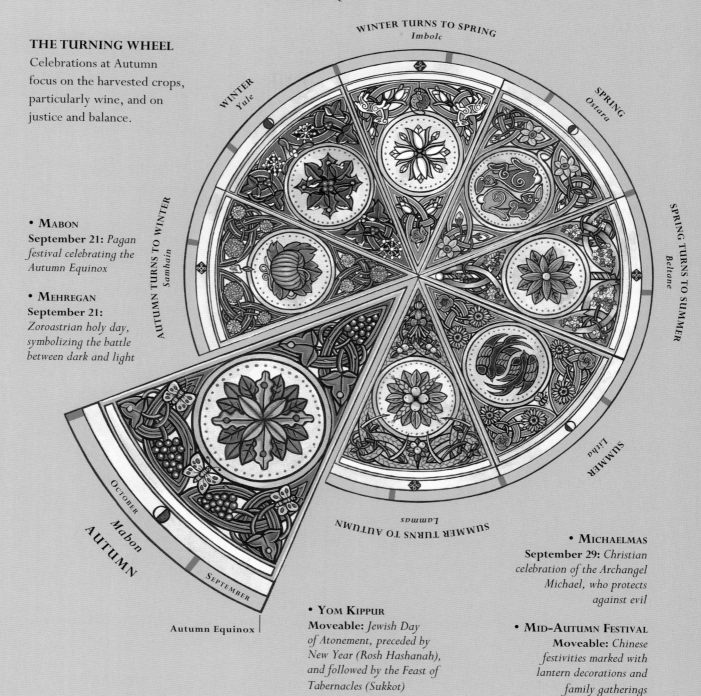

WINTER TURNS TO SPRING
Imbolc

WINTER
Yule

SPRING
Ostara

AUTUMN TURNS TO WINTER
Samhain

SPRING TURNS TO SUMMER
Beltane

SUMMER
Litha

SUMMER TURNS TO AUTUMN
Lammas

OCTOBER

SEPTEMBER

Mabon

AUTUMN

Autumn Equinox

- **MABON**
September 21: *Pagan
festival celebrating the
Autumn Equinox*

- **MEHREGAN**
September 21:
*Zoroastrian holy day,
symbolizing the battle
between dark and light*

- **YOM KIPPUR**
Moveable: *Jewish Day
of Atonement, preceded by
New Year (Rosh Hashanah),
and followed by the Feast of
Tabernacles (Sukkot)*

- **MICHAELMAS**
September 29: *Christian
celebration of the Archangel
Michael, who protects
against evil*

- **MID-AUTUMN FESTIVAL**
Moveable: *Chinese
festivities marked with
lantern decorations and
family gatherings*

101

Marking Equinox and Harvest

The Autumn Equinox and harvest festivals overlap in the ceremonial traditions of many diverse cultures. Symbols of the sun and thanksgiving rituals are important feature in many of these ceremonies.

• • • • •

As sunlight falls on the Mayan pyramid of Kulkulcan at Chichén Itzá, Mexico, it creates intricate patterns of light and shadow. On the Spring and Autumn equinoxes, the sun hits a corner of the pyramid in such a way that seven triangles appear on the staircase, imitating the body of a serpent undulating down the steps to meet its stone-carved head at the base. This represents the plumed serpent god, Kulkulcan, to whom the temple that surmounts the pyramid is dedicated.

Many other ancient monuments and tombs across the world have been planned according to where the sun rises or casts its shadow on the Autumn Equinox. Among them are Loughcrew Cairn in County Meath, Ireland, where sunlight travels into the main chamber on the equinoxes, to illuminate prehistoric sun symbols carved into the backstone of the chamber.

SUN AND HARVEST CEREMONIES

The end of the harvest was, and is, marked with ceremonies by many Native American tribes. The Cherokee held ceremonies to give thanks to all living things and gathered together in October at a festival (Nuwatiegwa) held in honour of the Great New Moon. They believed the Earth was created in this season, which is therefore taken to be the start of the new year. The tongue of a deer was wrapped and used in divination rituals, and there were also prophetic ceremonies involving crystals.

The Chumash of southern California celebrated the Autumn Equinox with a sun ceremony, which took place after the harvest had been stored. Tribal elders displayed mystical ritual objects (such as whale bones decorated with sun symbols), sang traditional songs and made speeches.

Prayers of thanksgiving and blessings bestowed on the community also play a large part in the Zoroastrian harvest festival of Mehregan, which is celebrated on the Autumn Equinox. Mehregan was recorded by the ancient Persians and is still celebrated in modern Iran. The festival was originally held during a month that was known as

Equinoctial sunlight and shade mimic the undulating body of a serpent on the staircase of El Castillo, a stepped pyramid at Chichén Itzá in Mexico.

Bagayadi or Bagayadish, to give thanks to the sun and creator-god Ahuramazda, who, Zoroastrians believe, brought light to the world at this time.

Rosh Hashanah to Sukkot

The end of harvest marks the end of one year and the beginning of the next in the Jewish tradition, ushering in an important period of festivities.

· · · · ·

Jewish New Year, known as Rosh Hashanah, is a two-day holiday which usually falls between September 5 and October 5. The festival commemorates and gives thanks for God's creation of the world. The *shofar* (ram's horn) is blown in synagogues, and people spend much of the day in prayer.

In the Book of Exodus, God tells Moses, "You shall observe ... the festival of ingathering at the turn of the year", with the result that Jewish New Year coincides with the harvest in Israel. The Hebrew word meaning "year's end" is *tequphah*, which can also be translated as "the equinox", linking New Year to this time.

A ten-day period of reflection follows Rosh Hashanah, culminating in the solemn Day of Atonement, Yom Kippur. This

A 13th-century manuscript illustration showing the ritual blowing of the shofar *(ram's horn).*

is a time of judgment and reckoning, when Jews confess and repent their sins, reflecting the themes of balance and justice common to many cultures at the time of the Autumn Equinox. Traditionally, a complete fast is kept from sunset on the previous day until sunset on Yom Kippur.

Five days after Yom Kippur, the more celebratory Feast of Tabernacles, also known as Sukkot, is observed. Sukkot was originally held to mark the end of harvest. In ancient Israel, during the harvest season farmers inhabited *sukkot* – temporary shelters or "tabernacles" – and today families erect versions of these shelters outside or adjoining their houses, in which they eat, entertain and, in warm climates, sleep, for the duration of the seven-day festival.

"*Autumn is a second Spring,*
when every leaf is a flower."

ALBERT CAMUS (1913–1960)

Moon Cakes and Lanterns

In the Far East, the Autumn Equinox celebrations are saturated with mythic and poetic resonances that to Western tastes seem appealingly evocative.

In Japan, both equinoxes (known as *Shunbun no hi*) are marked by six-day *higan* festivals, which last for three days either side of the event. *Higan* translates as "other shore", and worshippers repent past sins, pray for enlightenment, visit their family graves and reflect on perseverance, effort, meditation and wisdom – qualities needed, in the Buddhist tradition, to reach the "other shore" of nirvana.

AUTUMN IN CHINA

In China, the equinox is marked by the Mid-Autumn Festival. This is the biggest event of the year except for Chinese New Year, and a popular time for family reunions. The lavish feasts that are held feature *yuek beng* (moon cakes), ritual snacks made from lotus seed paste or red bean paste, which have been popular for centuries. In the 14th century, when China was invaded by the Yuan Dynasty Mongols, the Chinese passed messages of rebellion to one another hidden inside moon cakes, and the gathering tide of insurrection eventually overthrew the Mongols.

Another tradition, held on the eve of the Mid-Autumn Festival, has come to be known as the Lantern Festival. The name recalls a legend in which the emperor of heaven became angry with a village for killing his favourite goose. A fairy warned the villagers that he was planning to destroy them with a firestorm, and told them to light lanterns so that when the emperor looked down from heaven, he would think the village was already on fire. Today, children carry lanterns of all shapes, from simple spheres to birds, fish or dragons.

Paper lanterns for the Mid-Autumn Festival crowd a store in Hong Kong. Children take lanterns with them to evening celebrations in public parks.

Celebrating the Vines

For the Greeks, wine had its own god — Dionysus. All around the Mediterranean the harvest of the vineyard was a pledge of good living and good company.

• • • • •

In Mediterranean climates, the Autumn Equinox heralds the vine harvest. Grapes are picked and pressed to make wine that can be laid down over the Winter months. Vine imagery is common in the Bible, illustrating the importance of wine in Biblical times: in the Gospel of John, Jesus uses the metaphor of a vine to illustrate Christianity, saying "I am the true vine, and my Father is the vine grower", suggesting that God will look after his followers with the care needed to cultivate vines. Celebrations centred on wine were especially important in ancient Rome, which held the Country Dionysia at this time to honour Dionysus. This began with the harvesting and initial

Gods of Liberation and Danger

The gods Pan, Bacchus and Dionysus all have associations with hedonism, and with sometimes destructive, violent or sexual excesses among their followers. The image of a half-human, half-goat creature with a beard, horns and cloven hooves who encourages irresponsibility and evil became a common depiction of the Devil during Medieval times. Alcohol, and the gods associated with it, was seen as a liberator of inhibitions, and therefore a threat to urban civilizations, with their established moral and social structures.

pressing of the grapes. During the following month, festivities shifted to sanctuaries within the cities. The wine would then have its first tasting during the City Dionysia, a festival held in Spring, opposite the Country Dionysia in the Roman festive calendar.

The Roman equivalent of Dionysus was Bacchus, despite the fact that Bacchus is traditionally portrayed as a portly, drunken, slightly ridiculous figure, while Dionysus usually appears as a young, powerful divinity. The Romans also identified Bacchus with Liber, "the free one", an ancient Italian fertility god. Both Bacchus and Dionysus were associated with outdoor rituals attended by crowds of rowdy followers, as was Pan, the Roman god of woodlands, fields and fertility, who played pipes and protected flocks.

APPLES AND CIDER

North of the wine regions, hops for beer and apples for cider are harvested at this time of year. Many of the types of apple used for cider are too acidic to eat – so turning them into alcoholic drinks prevents them from being wasted. One piece of folklore prescribes that cider should only be made on the waning moon (just as the Autumn represents the waning of the

year) or else it will be sour. As late as the first decade of the 20th century, many farm labourers were paid partly in cider, and tradition dictated that they should pour a little of the drink onto the ground in thanks to the earth for providing the fruit.

This detail from a 15th-century manuscript shows the horned deity Pan in a verdant landscape, with vegetation growing from his pipes.

Dying Light

The Autumn Equinox, a milestone on the journey toward Winter, has many myths and legends associated with protector figures, who guard human beings and the natural world against the powers of darkness that come into play at this time of year.

• • • • •

In the Christian calendar, September 29 is Michaelmas Day, dedicated to Archangel Michael, who offers protection against darkness and evil. Michael, whose name in Hebrew translates as "Who is like God?", is one of the most powerful and important figures in Biblical tradition. He led the army of good angels against the renegade angel Lucifer when he revolted against God, and as a consequence of that battle, Lucifer was driven out of heaven. As St Michael, this heroic, sword-wielding figure was worshipped extensively in Normandy, Greece, Italy, and also in Germany, where

Praying for Rain

A region's climate or topography will sometimes have an effect on the way its myths are treated. For example, in an alternative version of the Babylonian myth of Tammuz and Ishtar (see pages 96–7), Tammuz, rather than being reborn in the Spring, is resurrected at the Autumn Equinox by the seasonal rains.

In this version of the legend, the period when he is dead corresponds to the hottest months at the end of Summer, when the strong Middle Eastern sun scorches the land and threatens to engulf it in desert. With the cooler weather and the rain, the plants revive and the survival of the people is assured.

Bathed in evening sunlight, St Michael's Tower stands on the summit of Glastonbury Tor in Somerset, England. The original church dated back to the 14th century.

he shared characteristics with the Pagan god Wotan (Odin), to whom many mountains were sacred. Mountain chapels dedicated to St Michael can still be found all over Germany. And a tower on the summit of Glastonbury Tor, in south-west England, is the only remains of a church that was once dedicated to him.

European farmers once celebrated the end of the harvest with a harvest supper eaten on Michaelmas Day, the centrepiece of which was a goose stuffed with apples. Traditionally, "goose fairs" were held during September, when geese and livestock that were surplus to Winter requirements would be sold, and farm workers hired for the months ahead. These fairs, which still take place in parts of Europe and the USA, were important to the rural economy, and Michaelmas was also one of the quarter-days on which rents and accounts were settled – an association that aligns with Autumn's themes of reckoning and balance, as seen in many celebrations at this time of year.

Autumn

TURNS TO

Winter

October 31 – December 20

"With sudden stir the startled forest sings
Winter's returning song . . ."

JOHN CLARE (1793–1864)

• • • • •

Twilight 114
Thanksgiving and Feasts of Plenty 116
Days and Nights of the Dead 118
Bonfire Nights 122
Diwali 126

Twilight

As November begins in the northern hemisphere, daylight is on the run, and darkness hard on its heels. In Celtic tradition, the shift from October to November is marked by Samhain, which translates as "summer's end".

· · · · ·

Samhain (pronounced Saow-en) marks the end of Summer, the "light half" of the year, and the beginning of Winter, the "dark half". For the Celts, this was a time of feasting and plenty, with parallels today in the American Thanksgiving festivities, which also take place in November. Pumpkins are used in Thanksgiving meals and for Hallowe'en lanterns, and their shape, a golden sphere, mimics the huge full moons that people seem to notice more in the Autumn. The Celts believed that ghosts could walk the Earth at Samhain, and late Autumn festivals accordingly tend to focus on the remembrance of the dead and the battle of good against evil.

Apple Traditions

Apples were celebrated at the Roman harvest festival of Pomonia, dedicated to the nature goddess Pomona. The fruit was also used in love divination rituals at Hallowe'en. Apple-bobbing was a popular medieval tradition – the first person to retrieve an apple from a bucket of water using only their mouth would be the next to marry. Young girls peeled the skin of an apple into a single ribbon and threw the skin over their shoulders – the shape it formed supposedly spelt the first letter of their future spouse's name.

THE TURNING WHEEL

Late Autumn and early Winter celebrations mark the end of the harvest and honour the dead, often with bonfires to enliven the lengthening nights.

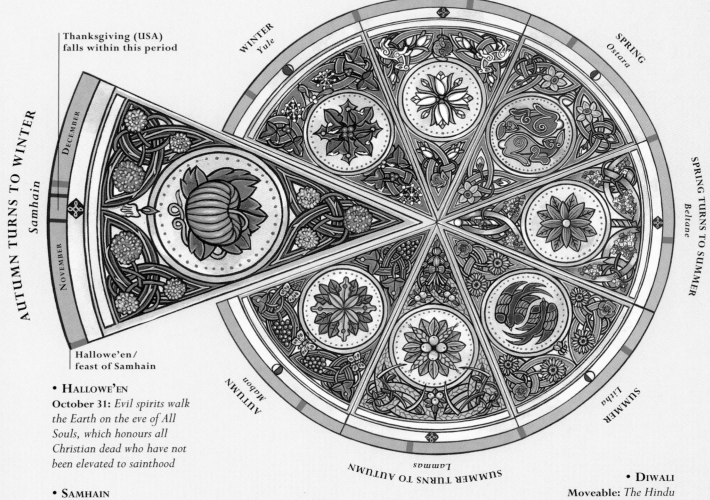

Thanksgiving (USA) falls within this period

WINTER TURNS TO SPRING
Imbolc

WINTER
Yule

SPRING
Ostara

AUTUMN TURNS TO WINTER
Samhain

DECEMBER

NOVEMBER

SPRING TURNS TO SUMMER
Beltane

Hallowe'en/ feast of Samhain

AUTUMN
Mabon

SUMMER
Litha

SUMMER TURNS TO AUTUMN
Lammas

• **HALLOWE'EN**
October 31: *Evil spirits walk the Earth on the eve of All Souls, which honours all Christian dead who have not been elevated to sainthood*

• **SAMHAIN**
October 31: *Celtic fire festival marking the Summer's end and the conclusion of the harvest season*

• **DAY OF THE DEAD**
November 2: *Latin American celebration to honour the sprits of deceased loved ones*

• **THANKSGIVING**
Moveable: *The fourth Thursday in November is Thanksgiving in the USA*

• **DIWALI**
Moveable: *The Hindu Festival of Lights, Diwali, which celebrates the Hindu New Year, falls in late October or in November*

Thanksgiving and Feasts of Plenty

Gratitude for the blessings of the earth runs deep and long: perhaps surprisingly, the world's best-known Thanksgiving festival takes place as late as the end of November.

• • • • •

Thanksgiving is perhaps the modern American calendar's most significant celebration. On the fourth Thursday in November, family and friends gather for a long weekend, to feast and count their blessings. Thanksgiving is a late celebration of "fruitful fields and healthful skies", as Abraham Lincoln put it in 1863 – but also, more generally, a time of gratitude for harmony, liberty and industry across the nation: in other words, plentiful blessings for a fortunate people.

Native American Festivities

The Cherokee month of the Harvest Moon (Duninudi) is followed in November by the month of the Trading Moon, or Nudadaequ. During this time, harvested crops, meat and skins from the hunt, and manufactured goods are traded between tribes as far afield as Canada and South America. The Adohuna, or Friendship Festival, takes place during the Nudadaequ, when new friends are made and business partnerships forged. Tribe members reflect on the nature of selfishness and greed, giving gifts to the poor and disadvantaged to help them through the Winter. It is also a time at which all sins but murder can be forgiven.

THE HISTORY OF THANKSGIVING

The Thanksgiving tradition originated in 1621 when the Plymouth Colony invited the local Wampanog tribe to celebrate their first harvest with them. The Native Americans had helped the early Pilgrims to plant crops and hunt in the unfamiliar landscape. For 200 years, Thanksgiving was marked on different dates in different states, whenever the harvest dictated. George Washington, as leader of the revolutionary forces, proclaimed a thanksgiving for December 1777 to honour the defeat of the British at Saratoga. Several presidents, including

This 19th-century lithograph depicts the familiar scene of a traveller returning home to his family to celebrate the festival of Thanksgiving.

Washington, declared specific holidays. President Lincoln encouraged the occasion as a means of national reconciliation after the Civil War, emphasizing shared heritage. In 1941, President Franklin D. Roosevelt signed a congressional bill fixing the date of Thanksgiving in American law.

Canadians celebrate it on the second Monday in October. As in the USA, festive meals tend to feature pumpkin pie.

Days and Nights of the Dead

As thoughts turn inward at the twilight of the year, remembrance of the dead features in many celebrations — from the Días de Los Muertos in Mexico, to Hallowe'en in Europe and North America, to Cheung Yeung in China.

· · · · ·

The idea of a November festival honouring the dead has ancient roots. At Samhain, according to the Celts, the boundaries between worlds were at their weakest and the spirits of the dead could return to Earth.

In farming communities, legend had it that the souls of deceased ancestors would return from the fields with the living farmers, and the living and dead would be welcomed together at the family hearth.

In Europe, festivals of the dead are still celebrated in many countries. In Lithuania, for example, the Velines, or Forefathers' Eve, takes place on November 1, honouring the spirits of ancestors. Lithuanian people prepare special feasts, light candles, visit the graves of their loved ones and give out food to the poor. Souls of the deceased who have not yet reached heaven are said to wander the Earth, following the paths toward churches in an attempt to navigate their way.

At the Christian celebration of All Hallows' Day (also known as All Saints' Day and All Souls' Day), every faithful soul who has not been elevated to sainthood is remembered and prayed for. All Hallows' Day falls on November 1, and Hallowe'en, which takes place on October 31, is seen as the night on which evil spirits have their last fling before the good spirits arrive to chase them away the next day.

LOS MUERTOS

In Mexico today, Catholic meanings attached to Hallowe'en have been mixed with traditions from the Aztec world. The journey to the Aztec Underworld was

A cemetery is engulfed in colourful flowers at Pátzcuaro in Mexico. On November 1, the local community stay up all night elaborately decorating grave sites, praying, eating and drinking.

Sugar candies in the shape of skulls are piled up at a store in Oaxaca City, Mexico. Candies such as these encourage a more fearless attitude to death.

fraught with peril. If the soul survived the journey, it could attempt to bribe the skeletal gods who presided over the Underworld to secure privileged treatment. The Aztecs set aside the ninth month of the Nahuatl calendar to honour the souls of dead children and the tenth month to honour adults, with abundant offerings and lavish fiestas.

However, under the Catholic rule of the Spanish *conquistadores*, the two months of celebrations were compressed into two days: All Saints' Day and All Souls' Day, which fell on the first two days of November. Today,

children are remembered on November 1 and adults on November 2, in carnivalesque, joyful occasions known as the Días de Los Muertos (Days of the Dead). Inside Mexican homes, families set up altars and surround photos of their late loved ones with flowers. Mexicans visit cemeteries to honour their ancestors and spend time with them. They say prayers, eat, drink and decorate graves

Autumn Remembrance

Chinese people consider it a duty to honour the dead through ceremonies, offerings and festivals. There are three major occasions. The first is Yue Lan, the Hungry Ghosts Festival (see page 86). The second is Chung Yeung, the Autumn Remembrance, which usually falls around the first week of November. This is a day on which to remember ancestors, visit family graves and pay respect to the dead. The festival originates from a 3rd-century Han Dynasty legend, in which a fortune-teller advised a man named Woon King to take his family to a high place for the entire ninth day of the ninth moon. He returned to find that every living thing in his village had been killed. The last of the three festivals is Ching Ming, the festival of Pure Brightness, which falls opposite Chung Yeung, usually in April.

with candles, incense and flowers, including marigolds (a sacred flower to the Aztecs, who called them *tzempazuchil*).

THE TWO FEASTS

The children's feast is known as the Little Day of the Dead. It features fruit, sugared pumpkin water, toys and candles, left out all night for the spirits; families share their meal with them by eating the leftovers next morning. The adults' meal on November 2, the Day of the Dead, is more substantial, featuring tequila and cigarettes, as well as *pan de muerto*, a bread covered with strips of dough made to look like bones.

Both feasts also feature small "death figures" of marzipan, and sugar skulls on which people's names are written, which people eat to prove they are unafraid of death. Tables are also decorated with skeleton dolls, including figures of wedding couples, beggars, musicians and soccer players. Known as *calaveras*, these dolls are symbols of resurrection and a way of introducing children to the idea of death without frightening them too much.

Bonfire Nights

Festivals in November often feature bonfires, lighting up the late Autumn darkness and recalling tales of good overcoming evil — or the defeat of political enemies.

• • • • •

Samhain was one of the two major Celtic fire festivals, on which people lit bonfires to celebrate, and to frighten away evil spirits. Farming communities brought their animals down from the fields into barns to protect them during the Winter months. As they left the fields, cattle were driven through purifying "balefires" (made from bales of hay), to burn off parasites and prevent the spread of disease, mirroring the cleansing ritual that takes place at Beltane. Old and weak animals were slaughtered so that food was not wasted on them, and this provided people with abundant meat for the Samhain feasts.

The cleansing properties of the fires gave them an association with ritual purification: in parts of Scotland, youths would light torches from the bonfires and run around field boundaries to protect animals and people from the malevolent spirits and fairies who were thought to walk the Earth at Samhain.

Villagers extinguished their domestic fires and relit them from the bonfires, ritually bonding families together for the difficult months of the Winter, when they might need to turn to one another for support. People also believed that the bonfires themselves, set on hilltops, would frighten away evil spirits and ensure a prosperous New Year. In Wales, people threw stones into the flames, and if these could later be found among the ashes, this was a sign of good luck for the coming year.

FIREWORKS NIGHT

Bonfire Night in Britain, which is held on November 5, is also known as Fireworks Night and Guy Fawkes' Night. It celebrates the failure of the Gunpowder Plot, an attempt by Guy Fawkes and a group of pro-Catholic conspirators to provoke a revolution by blowing up the Houses of Parliament. Their aim was to destroy the

English government and assassinate King James I and a large portion of the ruling aristocracy; but the conspirators were betrayed, captured, tried and executed. A feature of modern celebrations is therefore the burning of an effigy of Fawkes (known as a "guy") at the summit of bonfires.

Until the middle of the 19th century, November 5 was an occasion for young men to indulge in an evening of licence, but gradually more organized "bonfire societies" emerged, and the resulting festival became

Hollowed out pumpkins carved with faces — called Jack o'Lanterns — are set at the thresholds of houses at Hallowe'en to scare away the evil spirits.

less raucous and more elaborate, with features such as floats, effigies and lavish firework displays.

THE ORIGINS OF TRICK-OR-TREAT

At Hallowe'en, many children dress up as ghosts and witches and knock on doors asking for sweets and other gifts; if they are refused, they play a trick on the householder. The origin of the trick-or-treat tradition is thought to lie in the Christian practice of Soul-Caking, held on All Souls' Day (November 2), and widely recorded in the 17th century, although it is probably much older. Children would ask villagers for cakes in return for praying for the souls of departed loved ones; in some areas, the cakes were also given to the poor. Soul-Caking would often take place after an All Souls' Day carnival or parade, and the custom of wearing costumes may derive from participants coming directly from the parade. Short performances on the doorstep would often result in a more generous gift.

The practice of trick-or-treating and, in fact, Hallowe'en in any form, arrived in the USA with the large numbers of Irish immigrants following the Irish potato famine in the mid-19th century. Carving faces into pumpkins to place on the threshold to frighten away evil spirits also became popular at this time. Originally, root vegetables such as turnips were hollowed out, but pumpkins were soon found to be more easily carved, and in abundant supply in the New World.

Jack o' Lantern

Jack o'Lanterns originated in Ireland in the tale of "Stingy Jack". A sinful man, Jack was so drunk one night that his soul left his body. When the Devil appeared to claim it, Jack begged for one last drink. The Devil agreed, if he could have a drink too. Jack persuaded the Devil to turn into a sixpence to pay for the drinks, then quickly scored a cross into the coin, trapping the Devil inside. In exchange for his release, the Devil agreed to leave Jack alone for a year. When the Devil returned a year later, Jack tricked him into climbing an apple tree and scored a cross in the trunk, this time securing a promise from the Devil never to bother Jack again. However, when Jack died, he found that God would not let him enter heaven, so he was doomed to wander the Earth for ever. He therefore begged a single ember from hell to light his way and placed it for safety in a hollowed-out turnip.

"*I saw old Autumn in the misty morn,*
Stand shadowless like silence listening to silence."

THOMAS HOOD (1799–1845)

Diwali

The Festival of Lights, Diwali, marking Hindu, Sikh and Jain New Year,
is celebrated throughout the Indian subcontinent, Europe and America.

• • • • •

Diwali translates literally as "rows of lighted lamps" and is also known as the Festival of Lights. The most striking aspect of the celebrations is the tiny lamps, called *diyas*, which are placed in windows and around courtyards and gardens. At places of pilgrimage, such as Varanasi in eastern India, lots of candles are floated down waterways.

The Diwali festivities last for five days. The festival is held during late October or early November on the new moon between the Hindu months of Asvina (September-October) and Kartika (October-November). This time represents a reaffirmation of hope, and focuses on friendship and goodwill. Families wear new clothes to signify a new start, and homes are cleaned and redecorated.

THE DIWALI MYTHS

The myths associated with Diwali differ according to the region. Northern India gives thanks for the return of the Hindu god and legendary king, Rama, to his home city of Ayodhya following years of exile. According to Hindu mythology, Rama defeated Ravana, the demon king of Ceylon, and freed his kidnapped consort, Sita, aided by his brother Lakshman and an army of animals including the monkey-god Hanuman (shown left with Rama). The divine king's people lit the first lamps and fireworks to welcome the royal party home, in a symbolic recreation of the sights and sounds of the battlefield. In Nepalese lore, the victory over evil is won by Krishna, who defeats Narakaasura, the cruel demon king of Assam; while in Gujarat, Diwali honours Lakshmi, the goddess of prosperity.

HOSPITALITY, HOPE AND FAMILY

The main traditions of each day of Diwali also vary slightly, although they follow a similar general pattern. On the first day, people draw decorative patterns (*rangolis*) of white and coloured powder on the ground outside their doors to welcome visitors. This is a good day to make purchases, particularly of gold and silver. The second day is dedicated to lights and prayers for a positive future. The third day, Diwali itself, falls on the new moon, so sparkling fireworks are set off in the dark sky, special sweets are eaten and lamps are lit. The fourth day of Diwali is the first of the New Year, when debts are settled and feuds forgiven. On the fifth day, affection between siblings is celebrated.

Diwali candles float on the river Ganges at Varanasi, India. Varanasi is especially sacred to Hindus, who view it as the centre of the cosmos, where gods gather alongside humans.

Winter

December 21 – January 31

"O Winter! . . . king of intimate delights,
fireside enjoyments, home-born happiness . . ."

WILLIAM COWPER (1731–1800)

• • • • •

Winter Solstice 130
The Light Returns 132
The Arrival of Father Christmas 134
Yule Logs and Christmas Trees 136
Chaos and Misrule 140
Renewing the Cycle 142
Winter and the Underworld 143

Winter Solstice

In December and January in the northern hemisphere, well above the Tropics, the days are short and the nights are long. Yet many traditions have evolved their most extravagant festivals at this time, including Christmas and Hanukkah.

· · · · ·

Falling on December 21, the Winter Solstice is the shortest day, the least productive time in nature's annual cycle. But the end of one cycle is the beginning of the next, which makes Midwinter a time to look forward in hope. January is named for Janus, the Roman god of doors and new beginnings, depicted with two faces, one looking backward, the other looking forward. In Winter, we have time to contemplate the year that is ending and plan for the future. Many religions consider this to be a deeply spiritual time. The lighting of the Hanukkah *menora* remembers the Talmud story of how a day's supply of non-consecrated oil miraculously kept burning for seven days.

Marking the Solstice

Prehistoric sites and circles of standing stones all over Britain and Ireland show evidence of alignment with the sun on the shortest day. At Newgrange in Ireland at sunrise on the Winter Solstice, a shaft of light passes down a 62-ft (19m) passage to illuminate the central chamber of the huge chambered mound. Long Meg, the tallest stone in the Maughanby stone circle, Cumbria, aligns with the setting sun on this day; while light passes down a passage from the entrance to the inside wall at Maes Howe tomb in mainland Orkney, Scotland.

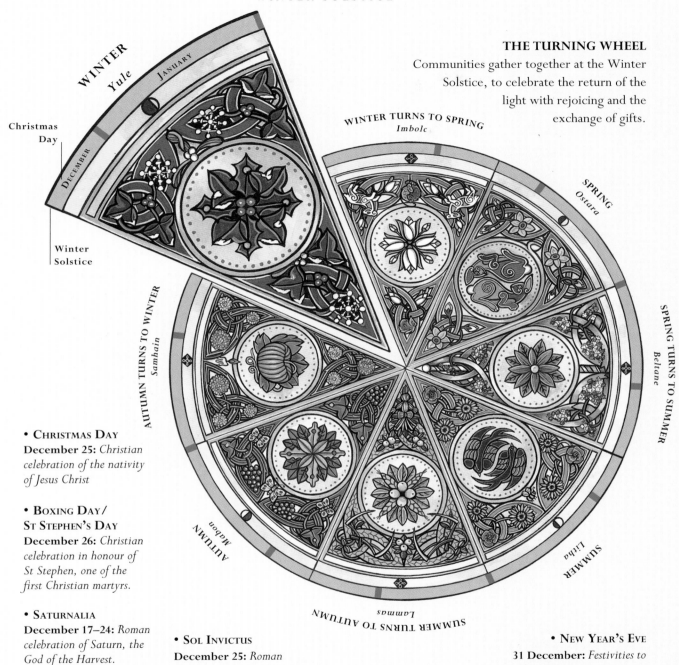

WINTER
Yule

JANUARY

DECEMBER

Christmas
Day

Winter
Solstice

THE TURNING WHEEL
Communities gather together at the Winter
Solstice, to celebrate the return of the
light with rejoicing and the
exchange of gifts.

WINTER TURNS TO SPRING
Imbolc

SPRING
Ostara

SPRING TURNS TO SUMMER
Beltane

AUTUMN TURNS TO WINTER
Samhain

AUTUMN
Mabon

SUMMER TURNS TO AUTUMN
Lammas

SUMMER
Litha

• **CHRISTMAS DAY**
December 25: *Christian*
celebration of the nativity
of Jesus Christ

• **BOXING DAY/**
ST STEPHEN'S DAY
December 26: *Christian*
celebration in honour of
St Stephen, one of the
first Christian martyrs.

• **SATURNALIA**
December 17–24: *Roman*
celebration of Saturn, the
God of the Harvest.
"Day of the Sun", the day
after the Winter Solstice

• **SOL INVICTUS**
December 25: *Roman*
festivities marking the return
of the "Unconquered Sun"

• **NEW YEAR'S EVE**
31 December: *Festivities to*
bid farewell to the old year in
the Western calendar

The Light Returns

One of the themes most strongly associated with the Winter Solstice across the world is the re-emergence of light out of darkness, bringing renewal of life and the promise of a successful future.

• • • • •

In ancient Persia, the longest night of the year represented the point at which the forces of darkness were at their peak, but the following day was known as Khoram Rooz, the "Day of the Sun". People kept fires burning through the night on the Winter Solstice and performed acts of charity. They also offered prayers to guarantee the sun's total victory, particularly to the god Mithra (see pages 50–51), who protected the light of the early morning.

THE UNCONQUERED SUN

When the Mithran cult appeared in Rome, the Romans named its Winter Solstice celebration Mithra Dies Natalis Sol Invicti (the Day of the Birth of the Unconquered Sun). Over time, this was shortened to Sol Invictus, the Unconquered Sun. These festivities became intertwined with the joyous rites surrounding Saturnalia (see page 140), creating an important festive period for the Romans. The main belief associated with Christmas today – the birth of a saviour who brings light to the world – is believed by some to be foreshadowed in the festival of Sol Invictus.

HANNUKAH

Lights also feature at Hannukah, the eight-day Jewish festival which marks the rededication of the temple of Jerusalem in 164BCE, and the later legend of the miracle of the oil (see page 130). Every Jewish household has a seven-candle *menora*, which is traditionally set up so that it is visible from outside the house. This allows passers-by to see the lights, remember the reason for the festival and share in the joy. Jewish families light a candle for each successive day, along with the central *shamash* candle, and celebrate with special foods and prayers.

Land of the Rising Sun

There are many exotic traditions which, although very distinct from the ways we celebrate Winter Solstice in the West, still mark the occasion as a key festival. Japan has Tohji-Taisai, the Shinto Grand Ceremony of the Winter Solstice. Japanese farmers light fires on mountain sides (including Mount Fuji, below) to welcome back the Rising Sun, the country's national symbol. Pumpkin is traditionally eaten with soy and miso sauces, as the shape and colour of the vegetable resembles the sun. Shinto is an ancient nature religion, to which the sun is central: the chief deity is Amaterasu, the sun goddess.

The Arrival of Father Christmas

The rotund, bewhiskered dispenser of good cheer we know as Father Christmas, Santa Claus or St Nicholas, who arrives in the dead of night on Christmas Eve bearing gifts for well-behaved children, is an amalgamation of several different seasonal figures.

• • • • •

Father Christmas's red clothes, benevolence and generosity to children have their origins in the legend of St Nicholas, a 4th-century Christian bishop known for his acts of charity. Little is known about the historical figure: it is thought that he was born in Asia Minor *c.*280CE, persecuted for his beliefs and imprisoned by the Emperor Diocletian, then freed by Emperor Constantine, who legalized Christianity. The cult of St Nicholas grew in importance, and he eventually became the patron saint of children, sailors and those in need. His saint's day is December 5 and is still celebrated by children in the Netherlands, Germany and other parts of northern Europe. Saint Nicholas is said to arrive by ship and then visits all good children, who leave their shoes by the fireside overnight and awake to find them full of sweets.

SANTA CLAUS

The name Santa Claus comes from Dutch traditions of Sint Nikolaas, or "Sinter Klaas". The modern version of Santa Claus appeared in the USA in the 1820s, following the publication of Clement Clarke Moore's poem *The Night before Christmas* (originally called *A Visit from St Nicholas*), which mentioned many of the traditions brought by immigrants to the USA such as the flying reindeer, the Christmas workshop and sacks filled with presents.

Today, St Nicholas is usually depicted wearing the red and white robes of a bishop or the green of renewal, linking him to the evergreen decorations of the season. Also dressed in green is the Pagan personification of the season, the Holly King, who rules this half of the year: he seizes power from the Oak King at the Winter Solstice. The Ghost of Christmas Present appears as the Holly King in Charles Dickens' *A Christmas Carol*.

FROM THE FAR NORTH

Father Christmas's elf helpers may also have their origins in the traditions imported to America from northern Europe. The Scandinavian *nisser*, the Finnish winter lads and the Swedish *tomton* were all mischievous house and farm spirits who rewarded householders who earned their gratitude.

The tradition of leaving out mince pies or milk and cookies for Santa (and even carrots for his reindeer) is a remnant of the time when Winter Solstice was primarily a festival of the dead in Europe: people would leave out food and drink for the souls that wandered the land on the longest night.

Symbolic Sacrifice

Celebration and symbolic sacrifice go hand in hand at this dark time of the year. The Feast of St Stephen on December 26 commemorates the martyrdom of the Christian saint, who, according to legend, was betrayed in his hiding place by a chirping wren. The custom of "hunting the wren", actually a cheerful house-to-house tour by parties carrying the wren and singing in return for hospitality, took place in Britain until the early 20th century. The Feast of the Holy Innocents (a reference to Herod's massacre) falls on December 28 in Catholic countries. In Spain, this day is known as *Santos Inocentes*, when people play pranks on their victims, the so-called *inocentes*.

Yule Logs and Christmas Trees

*Although bringing evergreens inside to embellish the house in Midwinter
may seem like a purely aesthetic contrivance, it does, in fact, have symbolic
associations — as do seasonal decorations such as mistletoe and stars.*

• • • • •

The decorated tree and Yule log that are central to Christmas festivities across the world echo the ancient custom of bringing evergreens indoors. Greenery protected the household, lending the benefit of its resilience during the coldest periods of the year, when life could be fragile.

Although it has usually become a chocolate cake in modern tradition, the Yule log was originally an oak branch. This wood was also chosen as it burns slowly but with great heat. When the log stopped burning, a portion was kept in the house throughout the year, for luck, and used as kindling for the next Yule fire. Red candles are often placed along a Yule cake, to represent the flames that rose from the log in the hearth. These candles migrated to the Christmas tree, and these, in more recent times, have been replaced by electric fairy lights.

TREE SYMBOLISM

Legend has it that when St Boniface felled an oak (sacred to Thor) in the 8th century (thereby "felling" Paganism), a fir tree grew from underneath the oak, and he dedicated this to Christ. Fir, pine and spruce trees are those we now most often bring inside to hang with shimmering decorations that catch the light, encouraging the sun back into the world.

The festival of Yule, among the Norse peoples of northern Europe, focused on the endurance of fir, holly, pine and other

evergreens. Many trees can grow from a single pine cone, giving the pine associations with potency, life and rebirth. The Christmas tree itself may also represent Yggdrasil, the Norse World Tree which linked heaven and Earth. Odin, father of the Norse gods, was called Jolnir in Norse, and this is one of the roots of the word "Yule". As Christianity spread west and north through Europe, it assimilated Yule into Christmas. Today Yule is more often the name for the Pagan celebration at the Winter Solstice.

CHRISTMAS STARS AND MISTLETOE

The star on top of the Christmas tree can be seen as the light of the sun, or as symbolic of the bright nativity star that led the magi to Jesus. There is no conclusive proof that a brighter than average star appeared in the skies above Bethlehem at the historical time of Christ's birth, but there were three contemporaneous occasions when Saturn and Jupiter formed a conjunction – appearing so close together that they might have appeared to be a single, brilliant star.

Mistletoe was a magical plant in the folklore of the Celts, Romans and Greeks. Pliny says that it was put into the drinking water of cattle to ensure their fertility. A semi-

parasitic plant with evergreen leaves which usually grows on deciduous trees, mistletoe was combined with other evergreens into "kissing bushes" hung in rooms where people would frequently pass each other. As described by Washington Irving, young men had the privilege of kissing the girls beneath the bush, each time plucking a berry from it; when the berries were all plucked, the privilege ceased.

The custom of kissing under the mistletoe is also connected with a Norse myth, which tells of the goddess Frigg and her love for her son Balder. Fearing that Balder would be killed, Frigg secured promises from everything in the world that they would never harm him, except for a little mistletoe tree, which she thought was too young to take the vow. The trickster Loki discovered this oversight and made an arrow out of the mistletoe, which he gave to Balder's blind brother Hod. Thinking that the arrow would not harm the invulnerable Balder, Hod allowed Loki to guide his hand. The arrow struck Balder in the heart, and he died. Distraught, Frigg banished the mistletoe to the tops of the trees. When the gods brought Balder back to life, Frigg was so overjoyed that she decided to make mistletoe a symbol of love.

"Make thou my spirit pure and clear
As are the frosty skies."

ALFRED, LORD TENNYSON (1809–1892)

Chaos and Misrule

One notable theme that has run through Winter customs over the centuries is the temporary reversal of social hierarchy — a short-lived redistribution of privilege.

· · · · ·

The Persian month of Azar ended with the longest night of the year, and, with it, came a temporary abandonment of the usual social order. Dressed in white, the Persian king would change places with one of his subjects, who would be crowned in his place during elaborate street parties.

Similar rituals marked the feast of Saturnalia for the ancient Romans, a festival at which they honoured Saturn, their god of agriculture. During Saturnalia, when quarrels and grudges were forgotten and people exchanged presents and lit candles to chase away the darkness, everyday conventions and roles were laid aside or deliberately reversed — masters and slaves became equals; senators, who usually dressed in elaborate togas, wore simple tunics; and men dressed as women — a precursor of today's pantomime dames.

In Tudor and Stuart times in Britain, an elected Lord of Misrule presided over feasts and entertainment in colleges and Inns of Court. He would often be known as "Captain Christmas" or "Prince Christmas" — one of the earliest records of a personification of Christmas in this country.

DARK SPIRITS ABROAD

Troops of spirits roaming at night, such as the *Cwm Annwn*, the hounds of the Otherworld, in Wales, are another manifestation of

Boy Bishops

In medieval Europe, a variation of the Lord of Misrule was the Boy (or Bairn) Bishop, who would be chosen, usually from the cathedral choir, and proclaimed bishop for a day during Christmas celebrations. Dressed in full bishop's regalia, including mitre and robes, he would process with the other choirboys, in the clergy's place, and preside over the services for a limited period. In some areas of England, the Boy Bishop would also tour the surrounding area with his retinue, visiting the houses of clergy and collecting money from his hosts and from spectators. In England, the custom was abolished by Henry VIII as part of ecclesiastical changes related to the English Reformation, but it has recently been revived as a Christmas tradition in some British cathedrals, including Hereford and Salisbury.

chaos associated with Winter. In Greece, the *kallikantzari*, unpleasant creatures which wore iron boots to kick people with, and made food go bad, are especially threatening in the 12 days after Christmas. On January 15, Epiphany, Greek priests used incense to cleanse villages of these monsters.

In the widespread legend of the Wild Hunt, lost souls ride furiously across the sky on stormy nights chasing a white stag, and bringing great misfortune to anyone who sees them. The leader of the Wild Hunt varies by tradition – for example, in the Norse lands, it is Odin; in France, Harlequin.

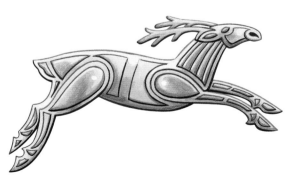
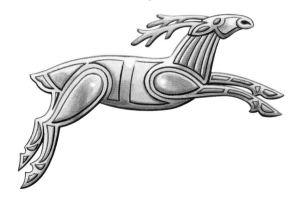

Renewing the Cycle

At the start of the year, many communities like to symbolically cleanse and "renew" themselves. The occasion is marked with rituals of resolution, purification and the welcoming in of the coming twelve months.

• • • • •

Early January is often seen as a time of cleansing, when it is possible for us to put mistakes behind us and make a new start. This is apparent in the modern tradition of making New Year's resolutions, to improve our behaviour or banish bad habits for the coming year. In Native American custom, January is the month of the Cold Moon. People fast to purify body and spirit, and prepare for the coming season; tools for ploughing are repaired and new ones are made.

NEW YEAR LUCK

In the British Isles, the first "event" of the year was often considered an omen for the months that followed. In a ceremony known as first-footing, people visit their neighbours after midnight on December 31, to wish them well for the year. The level of "luck" bestowed traditionally depends on the looks and actions of the visitors — on the whole, dark-haired men were luckiest, while red-haired women were especially unlucky. People with favoured colouring go from house to house (accompanied by less favoured companions), knock on the door and cross the threshold with a gift of food or light. They are rewarded with food and drink to cement the luck for the household, then everyone moves on to another house to continue the process.

Elsewhere in Europe, people "let in the year" for luck by opening a door or window at the moment of New Year, usually signalled by church bells or, in many parts of Germany and Austria, by trumpets being blown from the town hall (or church) tower. Sometimes people collected what was called the "first water" (usually drawn from a nearby stream or well) in order to bring health to their livestock and children.

Winter and the Underworld

In many traditions, the Underworld is a barren, icy realm, from which gods are banished — and therefore a natural equivalent of our Winter.

· · · · ·

In Pagan belief, the cold Winter soil is the final resting place of the vegetation spirit, who died or was sacrificed with the last sheaf at the harvest. He rests and regenerates in the earth during Winter, until he is reborn at the Spring Equinox. In some pre-Christian religions, the Underworld is a land of frost and snow, such as the Norse realm of Niflheim.

In ancient Greek myth, Persephone, daughter of Demeter, goddess of corn and fertility (see page 88), was kidnapped by Hades, god of the Underworld, to be his queen. While Persephone was trapped in the nether world, her mother's grief was so great that plants could not grow, and never-ending Winter seized the Earth. Eventually, the gods agreed that Persephone could return to her mother for half the year, and Demeter's joy brought the Spring. But when Persephone had to return to her husband, the world once again descended into Winter.

This 5th-century Roman terracotta relief depicts Persephone and her husband Hades, seated on their thrones as king and queen of the Underworld.

Zodiac Months

Astrology charts the movements of the sun, moon and the visible planets (Mercury, Venus, Mars, Jupiter and Saturn), through 12 constellations (the zodiac) which are ranged along the plane of the ecliptic.

Both the ancient Mayans and Egyptians observed astrological calendars, and the modern zodiac originated in Babylon. Tablets dating from the 7th century BCE attribute influence over human life to four deities: the sun, the moon, Venus and the weather god, Adad. These principles permeated other cultures including Middle Eastern, Indian and Chinese. In the 2nd century CE, the Greek astronomer Ptolemy named the constellations as we know them today. Most of the constellations in the zodiac circle bear the names of animals, so the Greeks named it *zodiakos kyklos* ("circle of animals").

Today, owing to "precession" (the wobble of the Earth's axis over millennia), the sun does not appear in the precise constellation that the zodiac sign ascribed to a particular date would suggest – for example, on January 1 the sun aligns with Sagittarius rather than Capricorn.

ARIES ♈ **starts March 21**
Named for Ares, Greek god of war, and represented by a ram, Aries is a Fire sign, strong and vigorous. The constellation's brightest star is Hamal, the "Horn Star" or "Ram's Eye".

TAURUS ♉ **starts April 20**
Taurus is an Earth sign, represented by the bull. The sign of Taurus is earth-bound, steady and reliable. Aldebaran is the brightest star in the constellation, which forms the "Eye of the Bull".

GEMINI ♊ **starts May 21**
The twin stars of Castor and Pollux mark out Gemini in the night sky. Gemini is an Air sign that has associations with adaptability, duality and opposites.

CANCER ♋ **starts June 21**
Cancer is a Water sign, sensitive and sociable. The constellation is an inconspicuous group made up of several small stars. The sun's arrival in the constellation of Cancer marked the Summer Solstice in ancient times.

LEO ♌ starts July 23

Leo is a Fire sign, symbolized by a lion. Proud and courageous, Leo is associated with the strong, steady heat of Midsummer. Regulus is the brightest star in the constellation of Leo, and one of the most easily recognizable stars in the night sky.

VIRGO ♍ starts August 23

Virgo, an analytical, energetic Earth sign, is often depicted as a woman holding a sheaf of corn, reflecting the harvest period into which this sign falls. The constellation is not easy to see, but its brightest star is Spica.

LIBRA ♎ starts September 23

Libra falls near the Autumn Equinox, when the days and nights are equally balanced: this sign is symbolized by a Justice figure holding a set of scales, or simply by scales alone. An Air sign, Libra is balanced between physical and spiritual realms. Its constellation is small and quite hard to see.

SCORPIO ♏ starts October 23

The brightest star in the constellation of Scorpio is Antares. This sign, symbolized by the stinging scorpion, has deathly associations, and in several cultures, festivals of the dead fall within the period of Scorpio. It is an intense, emotional Water sign.

SAGITTARIUS ♐ starts November 22

A more prominent constellation in the southern hemisphere than in the northern, Sagittarius is a Fire sign, represented by a centaur armed with a bow and arrow. The sign of Sagittarius is strong-willed and purposeful, displaying the determination needed to survive this wintry period.

CAPRICORN ♑ starts December 21

The constellation of Capricorn has no bright stars. Capricorn was originally symbolized by the wise, mythical goat-fish; today it is usually a mountain goat. An Earth sign, Capricorn is self-disciplined and stable.

AQUARIUS ♒ starts January 20

The constellation of Aquarius was identified by ancient Egyptian and Mesopotamian astrologers. Its brightest star is the reddish Fomalhaut. Aquarius is an Air sign, compassionate and visionary, represented by a man pouring out a pitcher of water.

PISCES ♓ starts February 19

Pisces, a dreamy, adaptable Water sign, is the last sign of the zodiac. The constellation is a diffuse group of faint stars, which has been represented since Babylonian times as two fishes, tied together by a cord knotted at the main star of Al Rischa.

The Tree Calendar

The "Tree Calendar" is a lunar calendar with 13 divisions. Modern Pagans use fixed dates for the "Moons", rather than measuring them by actual full moons, as this would eventually shift the months out of synchronization with the Gregorian calendar (also, in some years there are only 12 full moons).

The modern tree calendar has its roots in the 14th-century idea that each letter in the ancient Celtic alphabet was named for a tree. This was elaborated by the 16th-century Irish writer Roderic O'Flaherty, and repeated in Robert Graves' influential book, *The White Goddess*.

BIRCH MOON
December 24 – January 20
Birch, the first tree to grow back after an area of woodland is burned, is linked with rebirth and regeneration. Silver birch bark reflects the moonlight on Winter nights.

ROWAN MOON
January 21 – February 17
Modern Pagans associate the Rowan tree with Brighid, a goddess representing protection and purity, who is worshipped at the festival of Imbolc on February 1.

ASH MOON
February 18 – March 17
In Scandinavian myth, Yggdrasil, the World Tree, was an ash tree, and the first man was created from ash wood. Odin's spear was always made of wood from the ash tree.

ALDER MOON
March 18 – April 14
The Spring Equinox falls in the month of the Alder Moon. The tree represents balance, because it grows on river banks with its roots in the water and its branches in the air, bridging the realms of heaven and Earth.

WILLOW MOON
April 15 – May 12
The period of the Willow Moon is often the wettest of the year in northern Europe, and this gives the willow, which always grows near water, its associations with this period. It is also linked to healing.

HAWTHORN MOON
May 13 – June 9

May (hawthorn) blossom is abundant at this time of year, and people used to bring branches of it into their houses. In European folklore, gateways to the fairy world lie in hawthorn trunks, and several May traditions involve fairies crossing into the human realm.

OAK MOON
June 10 – July 7

The oak is personified as the Oak King, who rules the Summer. The tree was sacred to the Druids, and meetings were often held beneath its branches, which provided shade from the hot Midsummer sun.

HOLLY MOON
July 8 – August 4

Holly is the counterpart to the oak, which ruled the previous month. An evergreen plant, holly serves as a reminder of hope and the immortality of nature.

HAZEL MOON
August 5 – September 1

Hazel rules the period of the year when nuts are first appearing on the trees and can be added to the harvest. In Celtic tradition, hazelnuts were associated with wisdom and protection against lightning.

VINE MOON
September 2 – September 29

The Vine Moon rules over the period of the grape harvest in Mediterranean climes, and the blackberry harvests in the colder north. These fruits are used to make wine, and the period is associated with celebration.

IVY MOON
September 30 – October 27

The Ivy Moon falls at the end of the harvest season. It is an extremely resilient plant that often grows on dying trees. It can therefore be seen as a reminder that as one agricultural cycle ends, another will begin.

REED MOON
October 28 – November 24

Reed wood was used to make arrows for hunting and is also used to make wind instruments, whose haunting sounds can be used to summon the souls of the dead from the Underworld.

ELDER MOON
November 25 – December 23

The close of the Elder Moon falls near the Winter Solstice, and this tree, appropriately, represents endings. Elders recover quickly from damage and this ability gives the tree associations with the emerging New Year.

Cherokee Moon Months

The Native North American Cherokee Nation inhabits the lands that now make up the eastern and south-eastern United States. The Cherokee lunar calendar, by which seasonal observances are set and celebrated in this culture, has also become extremely popular with modern Pagans.

The Ah-ni-yv-wi-ya, as the ancient Cherokee were known, celebrated 13 cycles or phases of the moon each year. Each month started and ended on a new moon. The seasonal round of ceremonies was essential for social cohesion and spiritual growth.

In years when there are only 12 new moons rather than 13, the middle month (the Corn in Tassel Moon) is omitted. Some modern Native American systems always omit this month and follow a 12-month cycle, to coincide with the Gregorian calendar.

COLD MOON
FIRST NEW MOON
Beginning on the first new moon in January, the Cold Moon is a time for introspection and preparation. Families repair tools and tell each other stories of their ancestors.

BONE MOON
SECOND NEW MOON
As winter food stores dwindle, people may need to gnaw on animal bones. A feast is held to commemorate the ancestors, who have places set for them at the table.

WIND MOON
THIRD NEW MOON
During this month, the strong spring winds strip away the dead wood and foliage to cleanse the land for the new season. It is the traditional start of the agricultural year, when the sowing cycle begins in the fields.

FLOWER MOON
FOURTH NEW MOON
This is the month when flowers are in full bloom. It is strongly associated with healing, as many remedies are made from flowers. It is also a traditional time for births.

PLANTING MOON
FIFTH NEW MOON
This is the main planting season of the agricultural year, during which families

prepare the fields and sow them with the seeds from the previous year. Plants sown at this time include squash, yams and beans.

GREEN CORN MOON
SIXTH NEW MOON

This month is marked by the sprouting of the green corn in the field. Communities prepare for the growing season and repair homes damaged during the Spring storms.

CORN IN TASSEL MOON
SEVENTH NEW MOON

During this month, the corn shows a tassel for the first time. This middle month of the year is sometimes omitted in calendars following a more date-based, 12-month year to coincide with the modern calendar.

RIPE CORN MOON
EIGHTH NEW MOON

This is the harvest month, in which the corn is ready to be harvested and the first foods of the planting season can be gathered in. Social events and sporting contests are held, as the days are long and warm.

FRUIT MOON
NINTH NEW MOON

This month marks the gathering-in of the second major harvest — fruits. Berries in particular are picked from bushes, trees and hedgerows. Herbs are also harvested.

NUT MOON
TENTH NEW MOON

Nuts, gathered in to supplement the winter stocks, are the last of the foods that can be harvested from plants. They are used in the baking of nut breads, popular at harvest feasts held during this period.

HARVEST MOON
ELEVENTH NEW MOON

This moon marks the end of the harvest and is named after the full moon that sets over the fields at this time of year. The end-of-harvest festival of Nowtequa is held.

HUNTING (OR TRADING) MOON
TWELFTH NEW MOON

By this time, if communities want to supplement their food stocks, they must hunt. This period is also sometimes known as the month of the Trading Moon.

SNOW MOON
THIRTEENTH NEW MOON

Characterized as the time when the first snows fall in the mountains, the Snow Man spirit brings the snow to cover the Earth, so that it can rest until the seasons are reborn.

Glossary

Words in **bold italic** type have their own entries in this glossary.

astrology The study of the position and movement of the planets, the sun and the moon in relation to the 12 constellations of the zodiac.

Attis A Greek vegetation god who died in the Autumn and was resurrected in the Spring.

Aztecs Native inhabitants of Central America prior to the arrival of Spanish invaders in the 16th century. They had an advanced religion and elaborate cities.

Baha'i A Persian religion popular today in India, the USA, Africa and South America. Followers of Baha'i believe that the history of humankind follows repeating cycles.

barley An important crop, particularly in Europe, which features in many myths and legends, such as those of the Greek goddess **Demeter**.

Beltane Celtic **fire festival** held on May 1. It represents the beginning of Summer, the "light half" of the year, and has survived into the modern calendar as May Day.

Buddhism An ancient Eastern religion based on the teachings of Gautama Buddha (c.563–483BCE), and centring on the practice of meditation. It is widespread in Tibet, China and East Asia.

Celts A group of peoples inhabiting western and central Europe during the first millennium BCE. Their religion and cultural practices have greatly influenced modern **Paganism**.

Cernunnos The Horned God, a nature deity in ancient Celtic religion. He is associated with fertility and vegetation.

Cherokee Native American tribe from south-east USA whose lunar calendar is popular with modern Pagans.

corn In Britain, "corn" is a generic term referring to small grain cereals (such as oats, rye and wheat). Usually it refers to wheat. However, in the USA, "corn" denotes the plant known as maize in Britain.

corn dolly A doll traditionally made from the first or last sheaf of corn to be harvested. It represented the spirit of the corn, which is cut down in the Autumn so that it can rest and regenerate during the Winter, and grow again in the Spring.

Demeter A harvest goddess in Greek tradition. Her absence for half the year to search for her kidnapped daughter Persephone, who is in the Underworld, results in the barren months of Winter.

Dionysus Greek god of wine, with similarities to the Roman deities Bacchus and Pan.

Diwali Hindu Festival of Light to mark the beginning of the year; it usually falls in early November on the boundary between Summer and Winter.

Druid A high priest of the Celtic people. Druidism in the modern world has become a religion in its own right.

Easter Spring festival, commemorating the crucifixion and celebrating the resurrection of Jesus Christ.

ecliptic An imaginary plane, centred on the sun, on which the planets of the solar system are all positioned.

effigies Dolls and statuettes representing humans or animals, which can be used as substitutes for living beings in sacrifices and other rituals.

Eostre Saxon goddess of the dawn, who is associated with the Spring, eggs and hares.

equinox Two annual 24-hour periods when day and night each last for 12 hours. The equinoxes fall on (approximately) March 21 and September 21.

evergreens Plants such as mistletoe, ivy and holly that do not shed their leaves during Winter. In many religions, these are associated with resilience or immortality and are therefore sacred.

fairies Mythical otherworldly beings with magical powers who can, in some circumstances, cross the boundaries between their own world and the human realm.

fire festivals Two Celtic festivals, *Beltane* (May 1) and *Samhain* (October 31), which divided the year into the "light half" and "dark half".

Glastonbury A village in western England that has long been a centre of Christian and Pagan religion and is now best known for the outdoor music festival held at Midsummer.

Green Man A leaf-fringed face, depictions of which appear in holy buildings, particularly churches; in modern May Day festivities, a popular figure who marries the May Queen; in Pagan tradition, a reinterpretation of ancient vegetation gods.

Hallowe'en October 31, All Hallows' Eve or All Souls', when ghosts and evil spirits walk the Earth.

Hanukkah Jewish festival, which takes place in Winter, marking the rededication of the temple in Jerusalem, and the "miracle of the oil".

harvest festival A celebration of the success of the harvest, which often coincides with the Autumn Equinox. In many traditions, harvest baskets are given to the elderly and poor on this day.

Hinduism One of the major religions of India, with followers throughout the world.

Holi Hindu Spring festival, celebrating various myths focusing on the victory of good over evil.

Holly King Modern Pagan figure who presides over the second half of the year, from Midsummer to Midwinter, and fights an eternal battle with the *Oak King*, who rules from Midwinter to Midsummer. Their constant struggle represents the cycle of the seasons.

Imbolc Celtic festival held on February 1, celebrating the birth of new lambs and the first growth of new plants.

Incas Native inhabitants of Peru, 12th–16th centuries. They built extraordinary temples, many of which align with the sun at key dates in the year, and they had an extensive knowledge of agriculture.

Jack-in-the-Green A medieval interpretation of the Spring vegetation god, often represented in May Day fairs and parades.

Judaism A major world faith which originated in ancient Israel. It is an ethical religion, based on following rules laid down by God.

Jupiter The father of the gods and men in Roman myth. His equivalent in Greek myth is *Zeus*.

Krishna A potent male deity in Hindu religion; he is the main character in the *Bhagavad Gita*.

Lammas A festival held at the beginning of August to celebrate the harvest. The name comes from "loaf mass", as bread made from the first grain to be harvested used to be produced for the church service or "mass".

Lent In Christianity, a 40-day period of fasting, to commemorate Jesus' fast in the wilderness.

Lugh A god of light in *Celtic* tradition celebrated at *Lughnasadh*.

Lughnasadh The Celtic festival held on August 1, to commemorate *Lugh*.

Mabon Modern Pagan name for the festival held on the Autumn Equinox, named for the legendary Celtic figure of the same name, who the Romans knew as Maponus.

maize Staple North and South American crop, associated with several important deities in Mayan, Aztec and Native American religions.

Maya Central American people of the first millennium CE who built complex cities and followed a solar calendar.

Midsummer The longest day of the year, which usually falls on June 21.

Midwinter The shortest day of the year, which usually falls on December 21.

Mithras An important god in the religions of ancient Persia (as Mithra), the *Roman Empire*, *Zoroastrianism* and *Hinduism*.

mystery religions Cults including those of *Mithras* and *Demeter*, worshipped in ancient Greece and Rome, whose practices were kept secret from non-initiates.

Nile Major river of Egypt, whose seasonal floods, on which Egyptian agriculture depended, inspired many legends associated with the gods.

Norse The name given to the people of Scandinavia before Christianization, *c.*1300CE. Their gods included *Odin* and *Thor*, and their mythology was based on the World Tree *Yggdrasil*, whose roots were in the Underworld and whose branches stretched to the realm of the gods.

oak A tree sacred to the *Druids*, which also has important associations in many other religions.

Oak King In modern Pagan belief, this is the ruler of the first half of the year, locked in an endless struggle with the *Holly King*.

Odin Father of the *Norse* gods, who watched over the Seven Realms.

Orkneys A group of islands off the north coast of Scotland that have a rich history and mythology.

Osiris Egyptian god of vegetation and later of death and rebirth, associated with the sacred cycle of growth and decay.

Paganism A term to indicate a religion based on the celebration of nature, in which "gods" are seen as aspects of the natural world.

Persephone Goddess of the Underworld in Greek mythology and daughter of the corn goddess *Demeter*. Also known as Kore and Proserpine.

precession The "wobble" of the Earth's axis, a movement akin to that of a gyroscope, formng a complete cycle over a period of 25,858 years. It causes the position of the stars in the sky (when viewed from the Earth) to change over millennia.

Robin Hood Heroic figure from British folklore, who robs the rich to give to the poor.

Roman Empire Mediterranean empire centred on Rome which reached its zenith *c.*100CE when it covered most of Europe and extended into Africa and the Middle East.

St John St John the Baptist, prophet, and cousin and early follower of Jesus. His festival falls just after the *Summer Solstice*.

St Valentine Legendary figure who married lovers in secret and who is commemorated on Valentine's Day, February 14.

Samhain (pronounced saow-in) Celtic *fire festival* marking the change from Summer to Winter – the start of the Pagan year. Celebrated on October 31.

Saturn The sixth planet of the Solar System and the farthest planet from Earth to be visible to the naked eye. Also, an important god of agriculture in the Roman pantheon.

solstice The longest or shortest day. There are two solstices: at *Midwinter*, the shortest day of the year, and at *Midsummer*, the longest day.

Stonehenge Prehistoric megalithic structure in Wiltshire, England, whose stones have various calendrical, solar and lunar alignments.

Summer Solstice The longest day of the year, falling on or close to June 21. Also known as Midsummer's Day.

Talmud One of the sacred texts of *Judaism*, based on the Mishnah of Judah ha Nasi, a compilation of Jewish oral tradition written *c.*200CE.

Thanksgiving An American holiday which originated as a celebration of the end of the harvest. It is held on the fourth Thursday in November.

Thor An important god in Norse mythology, the son of *Odin* and protector of Midgard (Earth).

Triple Goddess A Celtic deity who has three aspects: a virginal young girl (Maiden), fertile or pregnant woman (Mother) and wise old woman (Crone/Hag), representing the cycle of life and the different seasons of the year.

Tuatha de Danaan The gods of ancient Irish legend, who represent the forces of light. Their enemies are the Fomoiri, who represent darkness.

Underworld The realm of the dead in many religions, usually located beneath the Earth.

Valentine's Day A modern love festival held on February 14 and celebrated in many Western countries. It is a day on which admirers are encouraged to send anonymous love tokens.

Venus The goddess of love in the Roman pantheon. Also, the second planet from the sun, which is visible as a bright star at sunrise and sunset, and is known as the "Morning Star".

Vernal Equinox Another name for the Spring *Equinox*.

Walpurgisnacht A northern European celebration which falls on the eve of May 1, marked with the lighting of bonfires and by people dressing up as demons and witches.

Winter Solstice The shortest day and longest night of the year, falling on or close to December 21.

Yggdrasil The World Tree of Norse mythology. Its roots lay in the Underworld and its branches reached to Asgard, the realm of the gods. There were seven realms in total, with Midgard (Earth) in the middle.

Yule Pagan celebration of the Winter Solstice. Many aspects of the Yule celebrations, such as holly and ivy and the Yule log, are now also incorporated into Christmas.

Zeus Father of the gods in the Greek pantheon.

Zodiac A series of 12 constellations which can be viewed as a belt around the heavens extending 9° on either side of the *ecliptic*. The movements of these constellations are used in astrology.

Zoroastrianism A religion that originated in ancient Persia and is still popular today in areas of the Middle East and India.

Further Reading

Aveni, A. *Empires of Time*. New York: Kodasha International, 1989.

Cavendish, R. (ed.) *Mythology: An Illustrated Encyclopedia*. London: Orbis Publishing, 1980.

Clauss, M. (trans. R. Gordon) *The Roman Cult of Mithras*. Edinburgh: Edinburgh University Press, 2000.

Cotterell, A. (ed.) *The Penguin Encyclopedia of Ancient Civilisations*. London: Viking, 1980.

D'Este, S. *Artemis: Virgin Goddess of the Sun and Moon*. London: Avalonia Press, 2005.

D'Este, S. and Rankine, D. *Circle of Fire*. London: Avalonia Press, 2005.

Flood, G. *An Introduction to Hinduism*. Cambridge: Cambridge University Press, 1996.

Hawkes, J. *Early Britain*. London: Bracken Books, 1987.

Hutton, R. *Stations of the Sun*. Oxford: Oxford University Press, 1996.

Matthews, C. and Matthews, J. *Encyclopedia of Celtic Wisdom: A Celtic Shaman's Sourcebook*. London: Element, 1994.

Miller, D. (ed.) *Unwrapping Christmas*. Oxford: Clarendon Press, 1997.

Owen, T. *Customs and Traditions of Wales*. Cardiff: University of Wales Press, 1991.

Partridge, C. *The World's Religions*. Oxford: Lion Publishing, 1982.

Ritchie, A. *Scotland BC*. London: HMSO Books, 1988.

Sayer, C. and Carmichael, L. *The Skeleton at the Feast*. London: British Museum Press, 1991.

Santino, J. (ed.) *Halloween and Other Festivals of Life and Death*. Knoxville: Tennessee University Press, 1994.

Sanders, N.K. *Prehistoric Art in Europe*. London: Penguin Books, 1985.

Tenzin-Dolma, L. *Understanding the Planetary Myths*. London: Quantum, 2004.

Weston, J.L. *From Ritual to Romance*. Princeton: Princeton University Press, 1993.

Wa-Na-Nee-Che with Harvey, E. *White Eagle Medicine Wheel*. London: Connections Book Publishing, 1997.

Wood, J. *The Celts*. London: Duncan Baird Publishers, 1998.

Index

A

Adam and Eve 26
Adohuna (Friendship) Festival 116
Ahuramazda 103
Aker 75
alder 146
Alexander the Great 64
All Hallows' Day 119
All Saints' Day 119, 120
All Souls' Day 119, 120, 124
ancestor remembrance 86–7, 121
ancient Egypt
   lion symbols 74, 75
   Nile floods 96
ancient Greece
   Eleusinian Mysteries 85, 88
   Olympic Games 87
Anglo-Saxon calendar 20
Annunciation, Feast of the (Lady
   Day) 39, 44
apples
   and cider 109
   and Hallowe'en 114
Aquarius 145
Aries 41, 144
Arthurian legends 58, 61, 100
ash (tree) 146
astrological calendars 144
Attis 50–51
Autumn Equinox 17, 20, 48,
   100–103
   Far East celebrations 106–7
   and harvest festivals 102–3, 104,
   108
   protector figures 110–11
Aztecs

calendar 12, 13, 120
and Hallowe'en 119–20
harvest festival 85, 91

B

Babylonian calendar 12
Bacchus 108, 109
Balder 138
Balor of the Evil Eye 93
Bavaria 63
Bede, Venerable 20, 30, 42
Beecher, Henry Ward 71
Belenus 54
Beltane 11, 13, 18, 20, 21, 54–5,
   58
   and Cernunnos 62
   fairy legends 60
birch 146
bone 148
Bonfire Night 115, 122–3
Boniface, St 136
Boxing Day 131
Boy (Bairn) Bishops 141
Brighid's Cross 29
Brighid (St Bride) 18, 25, 28–9,
   146
Brittania (Brigantia) 28

C

Cailleach Bheur 28
calendars 9, 12–13, 14–15, 20
   astrological 144
   see also lunar calendars
Callanish standing stones 80

Camus, Albert 105
Cancer 76, 144
Candlemas 25, 26, 30–31, 33
Capricorn 145
Carroll, Lewis, *Alice in Wonderland* 44
Celtic festivals 11, 13, 18
   and the wheel of the year 20, 21
   see also Beltane; Imbolc; Lammas;
   Samhain
Ceres 87, 88
Cernunnos 62, 63
Charles, Duke of Orleans 35
Chaucer, Geoffrey 34
Cherokee Nation
   Green Corn Ceremony 91
   month of flowers 55, 56
   moon months 148–9
children, festivals of the dead for
   120, 121
Chinese festivals
   Ching Ming 121
   Chung Yeung (Autumn
   Remembrance) 121
   Mid Autumn 101, 106, 107
   New Year 32
   Yue Lan 86, 121
Christmas
   Father Christmas 134–5
   mistletoe 138
   stars 138
   trees 136–8
   and Twelfth Night 11
Christmas Day 9, 11, 131
cider 109
Clare, John 113
Claudius II, Emperor 35

closure, symbolic acts of 11
Coligny calendar 10
corn dollies 94–5
corn goddesses 88–90
Cowper, William 129
Creiddylad 58
Cro Magnon man 12
crop deities 88–91
Cybele, "Great Mother of the
  Gods" 50–51
Czech Republic, maypoles 63

D
daisies 38
dead, festivals of the 118–21
Demeter 88, 143
Denmark, Midsummer rituals 73,
  77
Dickens, Charles, *A Christmas Carol*
  135
Dionysus 108–9
Diwali 9–10, 115, 126–7
dragons 32
Druids 78, 81

E
Easter 39, 42–3
  date of 31, 42
Easter bunny 42, 44
Easter eggs 13, 42, 43
Easter lilies 44
ecliptic plane 74
Egypt *see* ancient Egypt
elder 147
Eleusinian Mysteries 85, 88
Eostre 20, 42, 43
Epiphany 141
equinoxes 16, 17, 20
  see also Autumn Equinox; Spring
    Equinox
Ezili 68, 69

F
Fabergé eggs 43
fairs 92, 111
fairy legends 58, 60
Fajada Butte 80
farewell to old seasons 11
farming year 9, 10, 18, 20
  February 24
  harvest 84–5
  Midsummer 73, 77
Father Christmas 134–5
Faunus 34
Fertile Crescent 12
Fetching in the May ceremony 64
Finland 73
fire festivals 10, 18
  Midsummer 70–71
  see also Samhain
Fireworks Night 122–3
first-footing 142
Flora 56
Florifertum 55, 56
flower festivals 11, 54, 55, 56
flowers
  daisies 38
  St John's Wort 77
  snowdrops 26–7
  wood anemones 48, 49
Fravashis 40
Frigg 138
Fuller, Thomas 83

G
Gabriel, Archangel 44
Gemini 144
Germany, Walpurgis Night 55, 59
Ghana, "Hooting at Hunger" Festival
  87
Glastonbury Abbey, Holy Thorn
  tree 61
Glastonbury Tor, St Michael's
  Tower 111

Goethe, *Faust* 59
Golden Fleece 41
goose fairs 111
Graves, Robert, *The White*
  Goddess 146
Greece
  kallikantzari 141
  see also ancient Greece
Green Man 64–5
Gregorian calendar 12, 13, 15, 146
Groundhog Day 25, 33
Guinevere, Queen 61
Gundestrup Cauldron 62, 63
Gunpowder Plot 122–3
Guy Fawkes Night 122–3
Gwayn ap Nudd 58
Gwythr ap Greidawl 58

H
Hades, god of the Underworld 143
Haiti 68, 69
Haji Firouz 40
Hallowe'en 9–10, 114, 115
  in Mexico 119–21
  trick or treat 123–4
Hannukah 130, 132
Hanuman 126
hares, March 43–4
harvest 84–5
  and the Autumn Equinox 102–3,
    108
  crop deities 88–91
  Jewish festivals 104
  Michaelmas Day supper 111
  sheaf traditions 11, 85, 94–5
Hawaii 54
hawthorn 60, 147
hazel 147
Hecate 88–90
Henry VIII, King 141
hibernation 33
Hindu festivals

Diwali 9–10, 115, 126–7
    Holi 39, 46, 47
Hippolytus 88
Holi 39, 46, 47
Holly King 78, 135
Holy Innocents, Feast of the 135
honeymoons 77
Hood, Thomas 125
"Hooting at Hunger" Festival 87
hounds of the Otherworld 140–41
Hungry Ghosts Festival 85, 86, 121

I

Imbolc 13, 18, 20, 21, 24–5, 28,
    146
Iran 40
Ireland
    Jack o'Lanterns 124
    Loughcrew Cairn 102
    Newgrange 130
    and St Brighid 28–9
Irving, Washington 138
Ishtar, Sumerian goddess 97, 110
Islam
    calendar 14
    Green Man in 64
ivy 100, 147

J

Jack o'Lanterns 124
Jack in the Green 64–5
Jani festival 72–3
Janus 130
Japan
    Hanami 54, 55, 56
    higan festivals 106
    Setsubun-sai 24
    Valentine's Day 35
    White Day 35
    Winter Solstice 133
Jason and the Golden Fleece 41

Jesus Christ
    and Candlemas 30, 31
    and Joseph of Arimathea 61
    Last Supper 42
    and Lent 31
    resurrection 13, 50
    and St Brighid 28–9
    vine metaphor 108
Jewish festivals 42, 101, 104, 130,
    132
John the Baptist 69, 72–3
Joseph of Arimathea 61
Judah, son of Jacob 75
Julian calendar 15
June weddings 77
Juno Luciana 47, 77
Justinian 30

K

Kawoni 55
Khoram Rooz 132
Kronos 87
Kulkulcan pyramid 102

L

Lady Day (Feast of the Annunciation)
    39, 44
Lammas 13, 18, 20, 21, 84, 85,
    100
    fairs 92
Lancelot 61
Lantern Festival 106
Lascaux cave paintings 12, 14
Latin America, Day of the Dead
    115
Latvia 72–3
leap years 15
Lemuria 58–9
Lent 31, 47
Leo 74, 145
Lewis, C.S., *Chronicles of Narnia* 75

Liber 109
Libra 100, 145
lilies, Easter 44
Lincoln, Abraham 116, 117
lion symbols 74, 75
Litha 20, 21, 69
Lithuania 119
Lords of Misrule 140, 141
Lucifer 110
Lugh, Celtic god 18, 85, 86, 92,
    93
Lughnasadh 18, 85, 86–7, 92–3
lunar calendars 12, 14–15
    Cherokee 148–9
    Coligny 10
    Tree 100, 146–7
lunar cycle 12, 15
lunisolar calendars 14, 14–15,
    15
Lupercalia 34

M

Mabon 20, 21, 100, 101
Maia 54, 58
maize 89, 90–91
Malory, Sir Thomas 53
March hares 43–4
Maree, Loch 93
Mars, Roman god 41, 78
Matronalia 39, 47
May Day 11, 54, 61, 64–5
May Games 62
May Queen 64
Maya
    calendar 12
    pyramids 102, 103
maypoles 63
Mehregan 101, 103
Mexico
    maize 89, 90–91
    see also Aztecs; Maya
Michaelmas Day 101, 110–11

Midnight Sun 73
Midsummer 20, 68, 69
    all-night vigils 72
    fires 70–72
    hair wreaths 72–3
    love rituals 77
    Nile floods 74
    Oak King/Holly King battle 78
    sunwheels 70
    see also Summer Solstice
mistletoe 138
Mithras 11, 50, 51, 132
moon calendars see lunar calendars
More, Sir Thomas 44
Mother's Day 39, 47
Mount Carmel, Feast of Our Lady
    of 68

N
Native American traditions
    Adohuna (Friendship) Festival 116
    Cold Moon month 142
    Dehaluyi 69, 76–7
    Knee Deep dance 56
    Nudalaequ (Trading Moon) 116
    sun and harvest ceremonies
        102–3
    Three Sisters crops 91
    see also Cherokee Nation; North
        America
New Year 142
New Year's Eve 131
Nicholas, St 134
Niflheim 143
The Night before Christmas 134–5
North America
    Groundhog Day 25, 33
    Hallowe'en 124
    Mother's Day 47
    Thanksgiving 115, 116–17
    see also Native American
        traditions

Noruz festival 39, 40, 43, 51
Nudalaequ (Trading Moon) 116
nuts 149

O
Oak King 78, 135
oak trees 78–9, 147
Odin 138
O'Flaherty, Roderic 146
Old Father Time 87
Olwen 61
Olympic Games (ancient) 87
Ops 87
Orkney Islands 48
Osiris 96–7
Ostara 20, 21, 39, 42–3
Ovid, Fasti 46–7, 58–9

P
Paganism 20
    Holly King 135
    Midsummer rituals 78
    Ostara 20, 21, 39, 42–3
    and St Brighid 28, 29
    Tree Calendar 100, 146–7
    and Winter 143
    and Yule 136, 138
Pan 108, 109
Passover 42
Patrick, St 28
Persephone 88, 143
Persepolis, Iran 40, 41
Persian Winter festivals 132,
    140
Pisces 145
Pliny the Elder 78, 138
Plutarch 96
Pomona 114
Prahlad 46
Ptolemy, Greek astronomer 144
pyramids 102, 103

R
rain, Babylonian myth of 110
Rama 126
Red Wednesday 40
reed 147
Regulus, star 74
Rilke, Rainer Maria 37
Robin Hood Games 62
Roman festivals 11
    Dionysia 108–9
    Florifertum 55, 56
    Hecate 88–90
    Lemuria 58–9
    Lupercalia 34
    Matronalia 39, 47
    Pomonia 114
    Saturnalia 131, 132, 140
    Sol Invictus 131, 132
    Veneralia 46–7
Romance of Alexander 64
Romulus and Remus 34
Roosevelt, Franklin D. 117
Rosh Hashanah (Jewish New Year)
    104
rowan 146
Russia 43, 73

S
Sagittarius 145
St John's Eve 69, 72–3
St John's Wort 77
St Stephen's Day 131, 135
Samhain 11, 13, 18, 100, 114,
    115, 118, 122
    and the Wheel of the Year 20, 21
Santa Claus 134–5
Santa Cruz 54
Saturn, Roman god 87
Saturnalia 131, 132, 140
Scorpio 145
Scotland
    Bonfire Nights 122